Literature & Thought
GOVERNMENT AND CURRENT EVENTS

THE THREE BRANCHES OF GOVERNMENT

Perfection Learning®

EDITORIAL DIRECTOR	Carol Francis
EXECUTIVE EDITOR	Jim Strickler
EDITORIAL TEAM	Andrea Stark, Sheri Cooper
ART DIRECTOR	Randy Messer
DESIGNER	Tobi Cunningham
IMAGE RESEARCH	Anjanette Houghtaling
COVER ART	Mike Aspengren
REVIEWERS	Debra Bortzfield, Debra Robinson

5 6 7 8 9 PP 18 17 16 15 14 13

94349

PB ISBN: 978-0-7891-8294-4
RLB ISBN: 978-1-61383-183-0

Printed in the United States of America

WHICH BRANCH IS MOST POWERFUL?

The question above is the essential question that you will consider as you read this book. The selections, activities, and organization of the book will lead you to think critically about this question and to develop a deeper understanding of how effective the Constitution is today.

CLUSTER ONE How well does Congress represent the people?
CRITICAL THINKING SKILL INFERRING INFORMATION

CLUSTER TWO What makes a president great?
CRITICAL THINKING SKILL EVALUATING ARGUMENTS

CLUSTER THREE How does the Supreme Court effect change?
CRITICAL THINKING SKILL SUMMARIZING KEY IDEAS

CLUSTER FOUR Thinking on Your Own
CRITICAL THINKING SKILL INTEGRATING SOURCES OF INFORMATION

Notice that the final cluster asks you to think independently about your answer to the essential question—Which branch is most powerful?

THE THREE BRANCHES OF GOVERNMENT

It matters **enormously**
to a successful democratic system like ours
that we have **three branches of government,**
each with some independence and
some control over the other two.
That's set out in the Constitution.

—Sandra Day O'Connor,

former Associate Justice of the

United States Supreme Court

TABLE OF CONTENTS

THE CONSTITUTIONAL STRUCTURE

The Constitution reflects compromises designed to prevent both tyranny and government weakness. These compromises resulted in a federal government with power divided among three branches—legislative, executive, and judicial. Each branch would have powers to check or balance the other two. Below are excerpts from the Constitution that set up this system and explanations of the text.

THE CONSTITUTION OF THE UNITED STATES

We the People of the United States, in Order to form a more perfect Union, establish Justice, insure domestic Tranquility, provide for the common defense, promote the general Welfare, and secure the Blessings of Liberty to ourselves and our Posterity, do ordain and establish this Constitution for the United States of America.

Article I

Section 1 All legislative Powers herein granted shall be vested in a Congress of the United States, which shall consist of a Senate and House of Representatives.

Section 2 The House of Representatives shall be composed of members chosen every second year by the people of the several states, and the electors in each state shall have the qualifications requisite for electors of the most numerous branch of the state legislature. . . .

Section 3 The Senate of the United States shall be composed of two Senators from each state . . .

Article I
The Legislative Branch

Section 1 The most intense debate at the Constitutional Convention in 1787 was over representation. Small states argued that all states were equal, so each one should have the same number of representatives. Larger states responded that they had more people and so should have more representatives. Finally, delegates compromised and created Congress with two houses.

Section 2 Today, the House of Representatives is made up of 435 elected members, divided among the 50 states in proportion to their population. Read about life in the House in "Dream in Color," pages 27–32.

Section 3 In the original Constitution, senators were elected by state legislatures. With the ratification of the Seventeenth Amendment in 1913, senators were chosen by popular vote. Read about life in the Senate in "The Courage to Compromise," pages 20–26; and "Life in the Senate," pages 33–37.

Section 8 The Congress shall have power to lay and collect taxes, duties, imposts and excises, to pay the debts and provide for the common defense and general welfare of the United States . . .

To borrow money on the credit of the United States . . .

To regulate commerce with foreign nations . . .

To establish a uniform rule of naturalization, and uniform laws on the subject of bankruptcies throughout the United States . . .

To coin money, regulate the value thereof, and of foreign coin, and fix the standard of weights and measures . . .

To provide for the punishment of counterfeiting . . .

To establish post offices and post roads . . .

To promote the progress of science and useful arts, by securing for limited times to authors and inventors the exclusive right to their respective writings and discoveries . . .

To constitute tribunals inferior to the Supreme Court . . .

To declare war, grant letters of marque and reprisal, and make rules concerning captures on land and water . . .

To raise and support armies . . .

To provide and maintain a navy . . .

To provide for calling forth the militia to execute the laws of the union, suppress insurrections and repel invasions . . .

To make all Laws which shall be necessary and proper for carrying into Execution the foregoing Powers, and all other Powers vested by this Constitution in the Government of the United States, or in any Department or Officer thereof.

Section 8 The Constitution goes into great detail about the powers of Congress. That is, until the final paragraph of section 8. This clause, known as "the elastic clause," gives Congress the power to make all necessary and proper laws for carrying out its responsibilities. People disagree on how broadly this clause should be interpreted. Some believe that it actually adds very little to the other powers listed. Others argue that it allows Congress to adapt to new technology and other changes in society.

Think About It

- What are the costs and benefits of having the legislative branch divided into two houses?

- Do you think the power granted Congress in the elastic clause is necessary, or dangerous, or both?

House Judiciary Committee Oversight Hearing

Article II

Section 1 The executive power shall be vested in a President of the United States of America. He shall hold his office during the term of four years, and, together with the Vice President, chosen for the same term . . .

Section 2 The President shall be commander in chief of the Army and Navy of the United States, and of the militia of the several states, when called into the actual service of the United States; he may require the opinion, in writing, of the principal officer in each of the executive departments, upon any subject relating to the duties of their respective offices, and he shall have power to grant reprieves and pardons for offenses against the United States, except in cases of impeachment.

He shall have power, by and with the advice and consent of the Senate, to make treaties, provided two thirds of the Senators present concur; and he shall nominate, and by and with the advice and consent of the Senate, shall appoint ambassadors, other public ministers and consuls, judges of the Supreme Court, and all other officers of the United States, whose appointments are not herein otherwise provided for, and which shall be established by law . . .

Article III

Section 1 The judicial power of the United States, shall be vested in one Supreme Court, and in such inferior courts as the Congress may from time to time ordain and establish. The judges, both of the supreme and inferior courts, shall hold their offices during good behavior . . .

Article II
The Executive Branch

Section 1 In monarchies, kings and queens govern because they are descended from the previous ruler. In republics, presidents and other leaders govern by authority of the people of the country. Read more about the life of a president in "Listen Up, Mr. President," pages 68–73.

Section 2 The Constitution gives the president wide powers in foreign affairs and expects the president and Congress to work together to pass laws.

Think About It

In many countries, the chief executive is chosen from the largest party in the legislature. What are the advantages and disadvantages of this system?

Article III
The Judicial Branch

Section 1 The Constitution protects justices from the pressures of public opinion. Instead of being elected, they are nominated by the president and confirmed by Congress. They serve until they choose to retire. Read about life on the Supreme Court in "Friends and Foes on the Supreme Court," pages 85–91.

Think About It

What are the advantages and disadvantages of lifetime appointments?

LANDMARKS IN THE SEPARATION OF POWERS

1768

Baron de Montesquieu publishes *The Spirit of Laws*.

A French noble argues that societies can prevent tyranny by separating the people who make the laws, those who enforce the laws, and those who judge whether someone has broken the law.

1796

President Washington establishes the principle of executive privilege.

Washington refuses a request by the House of Representatives for documents about a treaty. He argues that the Senate alone has the power to ratify treaties, so he turns over the documents to the Senate only.

1857

The Supreme Court declares a second congressional act unconstitutional.

In the Dred Scott case, the Supreme Court ruled that Congress acted improperly when it banned slavery in the territories in 1820.

1803

The Supreme Court rules a law unconstitutional for the first time.

In *Marbury v. Madison,* the Supreme Court, under Chief Justice John Marshall, rules that a congressional act granting certain powers to the Supreme Court violated the Constitution. This establishes the principle of judicial review.

1787

Delegates meet in Philadelphia and draft the Constitution.

They set up a system of checks and balances among three branches—legislative (Congress), executive (the President), and the judiciary (the Supreme Court).

1941

Congress declares war against Japan and President Franklin Roosevelt signs it.

The United States formally entered World War II. Though presidents have sent U.S. troops into major conflicts in Korea, Vietnam, Afghanistan, Iraq, and other places, Congress has not declared war since 1941.

1974

The Supreme Court orders President Nixon to release tape recordings of phone conversations about the Watergate scandal.

Although Nixon appeals to executive privilege, the Court decides that it is limited in a criminal prosecution. Four days after he turns over the tapes, Nixon resigns.

1998

The Supreme Court rules unconstitutional a law expanding the president's veto power.

In 1996, Congress gave the president the power to veto individual spending projects within a bill without vetoing the rest of the bill. The Supreme Court says this violates the principle that Congress, not the president, holds the power to spend money.

1973

Congress passes the War Powers Act.

Congress attempts to reassert its power to declare war by clarifying when presidents can send U.S. forces into dangerous situations.

1995

The Supreme Court overturns a congressional law banning guns near schools.

In *Lopez v. United States* and other decisions, the Court narrows the scope of what Congress can regulate as part of "interstate commerce."

The Three Branches

LEGISLATIVE BRANCH
(Congress)

Writes laws

Passes the federal budget

Confirms presidential
appointments
(Senate only)

Ratifies treaties
(Senate only)

EXECUTIVE BRANCH
(President)

Proposes laws

Commands the
armed forces

Conducts foreign policy

Carries out decisions by
Congress and the courts

JUDICIAL BRANCH
(Supreme Court)

Interprets the
Constitution

Judges constitutionality
of laws

Reviews lower-court
decisions

Checks and Balances

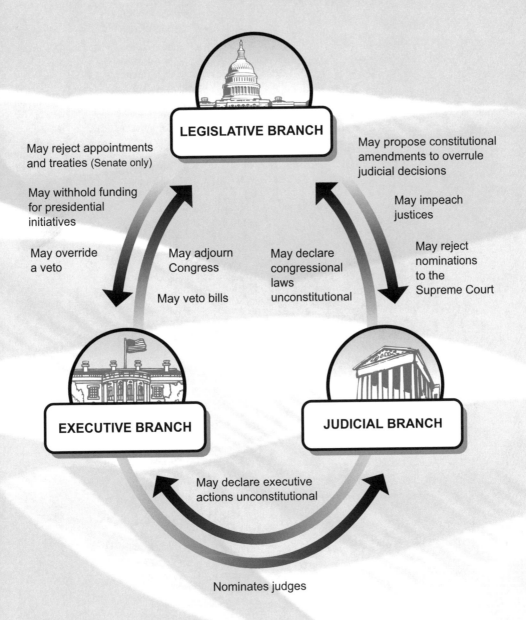

LEGISLATIVE BRANCH

May reject appointments
and treaties (Senate only)

May withhold funding
for presidential
initiatives

May override
a veto

May adjourn
Congress

May veto bills

May propose constitutional
amendments to overrule
judicial decisions

May impeach
justices

May reject
nominations
to the
Supreme Court

May declare
congressional
laws
unconstitutional

EXECUTIVE BRANCH

JUDICIAL BRANCH

May declare executive
actions unconstitutional

Nominates judges

GOVERNMENTS AROUND THE WORLD

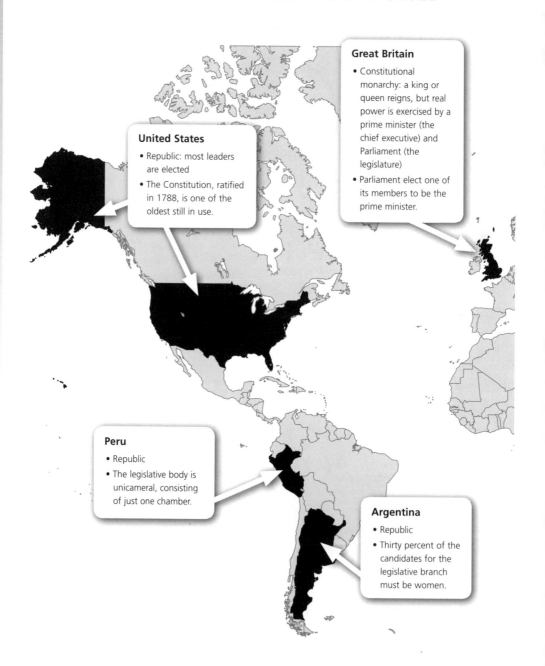

Great Britain
- Constitutional monarchy: a king or queen reigns, but real power is exercised by a prime minister (the chief executive) and Parliament (the legislature)
- Parliament elect one of its members to be the prime minister.

United States
- Republic: most leaders are elected
- The Constitution, ratified in 1788, is one of the oldest still in use.

Peru
- Republic
- The legislative body is unicameral, consisting of just one chamber.

Argentina
- Republic
- Thirty percent of the candidates for the legislative branch must be women.

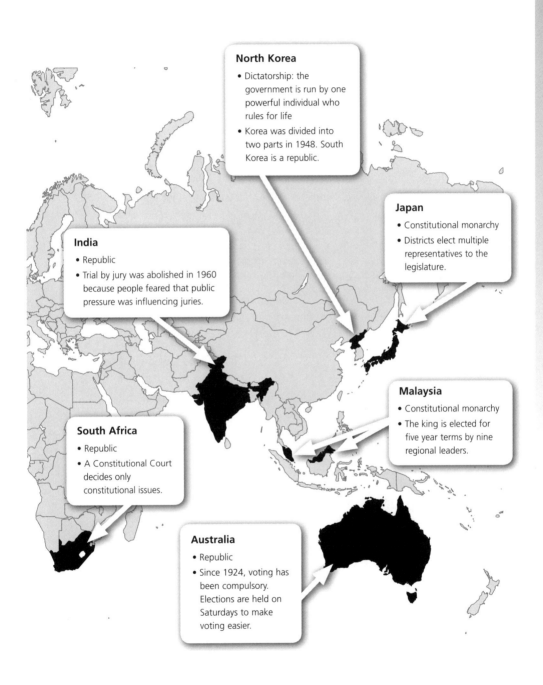

North Korea
- Dictatorship: the government is run by one powerful individual who rules for life
- Korea was divided into two parts in 1948. South Korea is a republic.

Japan
- Constitutional monarchy
- Districts elect multiple representatives to the legislature.

India
- Republic
- Trial by jury was abolished in 1960 because people feared that public pressure was influencing juries.

Malaysia
- Constitutional monarchy
- The king is elected for five year terms by nine regional leaders.

South Africa
- Republic
- A Constitutional Court decides only constitutional issues.

Australia
- Republic
- Since 1924, voting has been compulsory. Elections are held on Saturdays to make voting easier.

CONCEPT VOCABULARY

You will find the following terms and definitions useful as you read and discuss the selections in this book.

adjudication the process a judge uses to make a decision

appropriation an act by Congress or another legislative body that authorizes spending money

Beltway a nickname for the government in Washington, D.C.; it refers to Interstate 495, a highway that completely circles Washington, D.C., and is known as the Capital Beltway

bill a proposed law under consideration by Congress or another legislative body

cabal a group of people, often secretly trying to gain power

constitution the fundamental principles or laws of a country or state; in the United States, each state and the federal government has a written constitution, while countries such as Great Britain have unwritten constitutions

federal a system of government in which power is divided between a central government and state or local governments; it can also refer to the central government in such a system

gerrymandering drawing the borders of electoral districts to favor one part or particular candidate

habeas corpus the legal requirement that prevents the government from imprisoning a person without a charge

judicature the system of courts and judges

judicial review the power of a court to declare a law invalid because it violates the Constitution

jurisprudence a philosophy of law

magistracy the people who serve as judges

recusal the act of a judge removing himself or herself from deciding a case in which people might suspect they have personal reasons to favor one side

remand to send the case back to a lower court

republic a form of government in which the supreme power resides with the citizens, who elect representatives and other leaders to serve in government

spoils system the practice of appointing one's political supporters to government offices

tribunals judges and justices

CLUSTER ONE

How Well Does Congress Represent the People?

Critical Thinking Skill INFERRING INFORMATION

THE OLD HOUSE OF REPRESENTATIVES 1822 Samuel F. B. Morse

DANIEL WEBSTER 1894 Carl Conrads

THE COURAGE TO COMPROMISE

JOHN F. KENNEDY

Conflict over slavery threatened to destroy the United States in 1850. Hoping to preserve the Union, Kentucky Senator Henry Clay proposed a set of bills about slavery known as the Compromise of 1850. For Massachusetts Senator Daniel Webster, voting for the compromise went against his and his supporters' anti-slavery principles. Opposing the compromise, though, risked war. John Kennedy wrote this profile of Webster several years before he became president in 1960.

By the end of February, the Senator from Massachusetts had determined upon his course. Only the Clay Compromise, Daniel Webster decided, could avert secession and civil war; and he wrote a friend that he planned "to make an honest truth-telling speech and a Union speech, and discharge a clear conscience." As he set to work preparing his notes, he received abundant warning of the attacks his message would provoke. His constituents and Massachusetts newspapers admonished him strongly not to waver in his consistent anti-slavery stand, and many urged him to employ still tougher tones against the South. But the Senator from Massachusetts had made up his mind, as he told his friends on March 6, "to push my skiff[1] from the shore alone." He would act according to the creed with which he had challenged the Senate several years earlier:

"Inconsistencies of opinion arising from changes of circumstances are often justifiable. But there is one sort of inconsistency that is culpable:[2] it is the inconsistency between a man's conviction and his vote, between his conscience and his conduct. No man shall ever charge me with an inconsistency of that kind."

And so came the 7th of March, 1850, the only day in history which would become the title of a speech delivered on the Senate floor. No one recalls today—no one even recalled in 1851—the formal title Webster

---

1   **skiff:** a type of small boat with a flat bottom
2   **culpable:** deserving of criticism

gave his address, for it had become the "Seventh of March" speech as much as Independence Day is known as the Fourth of July.

Realizing after months of insomnia[3] that this might be the last great effort his health would permit, Webster stimulated his strength for the speech by oxide of arsenic and other drugs, and devoted the morning to polishing up his notes. He was excitedly interrupted by the Sergeant at Arms, who told him that even then—two hours before the Senate was to meet—the chamber, the galleries, the anterooms [waiting rooms] and even the corridors of the Capitol were filled with those who had been traveling for days from all parts of the nation to hear Daniel Webster. Many foreign diplomats and most of the House of Representatives were among those vying for standing room. As the Senate met, members could scarcely walk to their seats through the crowd of spectators and temporary seats made of public documents stacked on top of each other. Most Senators gave up their seats to ladies, and stood in the aisles awaiting Webster's opening blast.

As the Vice President's gavel commenced the session, Senator Walker of Wisconsin, who held the floor to finish a speech begun the day before, told the Chair that "this vast audience has not come to hear me, and there is but one man who can assemble such an audience. They expect to hear him, and I feel it is my duty, as it is my pleasure, to give the floor to the Senator from Massachusetts."

The crowd fell silent as Daniel Webster rose slowly to his feet, all the impressive powers of his extraordinary physical appearance—the great, dark, brooding eyes, the wonderfully bronzed complexion, the majestic domed forehead—commanding the same awe they had commanded for more than thirty years. Garbed in his familiar blue tailed coat with brass buttons, and a buff waistcoat and breeches, he deliberately paused a moment as he gazed about at the greatest assemblage of Senators ever to gather in that chamber—Clay, Benton, Houston, Jefferson Davis, Hale, Bell, Cass, Seward, Chase, Stephen A. Douglas and others. But one face was missing—that of the ailing John C. Calhoun.

All eyes were fixed on the speaker; no spectator save his own son knew what he would say. "I have never before," wrote a newspaper correspondent, "witnessed an occasion on which there was deeper feeling enlisted or more universal anxiety to catch the most distinct echo of the speaker's voice."

---

3 **insomnia:** difficulty sleeping

In his moments of magnificent inspiration, as Emerson once described him, Webster was truly "the great cannon loaded to the lips." Summoning for the last time that spellbinding oratorical[4] ability, he abandoned his previous opposition to slavery in the territories, abandoned his constituents' abhorrence[5] of the Fugitive Slave Law,[6] abandoned his own place in the history and hearts of his countrymen and abandoned his last chance for the goal that had eluded him for over twenty years— the Presidency. Daniel Webster preferred to risk his career and, his reputation rather than risk the Union.

"Mr. President," he began, "I wish to speak today, not as a Massachusetts man, nor as a Northern man, but as an American and a Member of the Senate of the United States. . . . I speak today for the preservation of the Union. Hear me for my cause."

He had spoken but for a short time when the gaunt,[7] bent form of Calhoun, wrapped in a black cloak, was dramatically assisted into his seat, where he sat trembling, scarcely able to move, and unnoticed by the speaker. After several expressions of regret by Webster that illness prevented the distinguished Senator from South Carolina from being present, Calhoun struggled up, grasping the arms of his chair, and in a clear and ghostly voice proudly announced, "The Senator from South Carolina *is* in his seat." Webster was touched, and with tears in

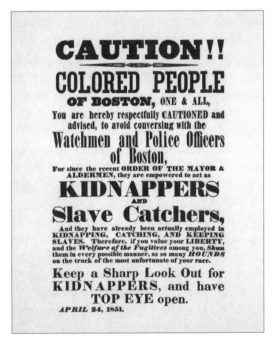

The Fugitive Slave Law forced people to decide whether to obey the law by helping capture escaped slaves. At times, slave catchers also tried to capture African Americans who were born free or who had purchased their freedom.

---

4 **oratorical:** related to public speaking
5 **abhorrence:** feeling of intense dislike
6 **Fugitive Slave Law:** a federal law requiring all citizens to help capture runaway slaves
7 **gaunt:** very thin

his eyes he extended a bow toward Calhoun, who sank back exhausted and feeble, eyeing the Massachusetts orator with a sphinx-like expression which disclosed no hint of either approval or disapproval.

For three hours and eleven minutes, with only a few references to his extensive notes, Daniel Webster pleaded the Union's cause. Relating the grievances of each side, he asked for conciliation and understanding in the name of patriotism. The Senate's main concern, he insisted, was neither to promote slavery nor to abolish it, but to preserve the United States of America. And with telling logic and remarkable foresight he bitterly attacked the idea of "peaceable secession":

"Sir, your eyes and mine are never destined to see that miracle. The dismemberment of this vast country without convulsion! Who is so foolish . . . as to expect to see any such thing? . . . Instead of speaking of the possibility or utility of secession, instead of dwelling in those caverns of darkness, . . . let us enjoy the fresh air of liberty and union. . . . Let us make our generation one of the strongest and brightest links in that golden chain which is destined, I fondly believe, to grapple the people of all the states to this Constitution for ages to come."

There was no applause. Buzzing and astonished whispering, yes, but no applause. Perhaps his hearers were too intent—or too astonished. A reporter rushed to the telegraph office. "Mr. Webster has assumed a great responsibility," he wired his paper, "and whether he succeeds or fails, the courage with which he has come forth at least entitles him to the respect of the country."

Daniel Webster did succeed. Even though his speech was repudiated by many in the North, the very fact that one who represented such a belligerent constituency would appeal for understanding in the name of unity and patriotism was recognized in Washington and throughout the South as a *bona fide*[8] assurance of Southern rights. Despite Calhoun's own intransigence,[9] his Charleston *Mercury* praised Webster's address as "noble in language, generous and conciliatory in tone. Mr. Calhoun's clear and powerful exposition[10] would have had something of a decisive effect if it had not been so soon followed by Mr. Webster's masterly playing." And the New Orleans *Picayune* hailed Webster for "the moral courage to do what he believes to be just in itself and necessary for the peace and safety of the country."

---

8   *bona fide:* a Latin phrase that means "genuine"

9   **intransigence:** unwillingness to compromise

10 **exposition:** speech; this refers to a Calhoun speech defending slaveowners' interests

And so the danger of immediate secession and bloodshed passed. As Senator Winthrop remarked, Webster's speech had "disarmed and quieted the South [and] knocked the Nashville Convention [a proslavery meeting in 1850] into a cocked hat."[11] The *Journal of Commerce* was to remark in later months that "Webster did more than any other man in the whole country, and at a greater hazard of personal popularity, to stem and roll back the torrent of sectionalism which in 1850 threatened to overthrow the pillars of the Constitution and the Union." . . .

But it was not understood by the Abolitionists and Free Soilers of 1850. Few politicians have had the distinction of being scourged by such talented constituents. The Rev. Theodore Parker, heedless of the dangers of secession, who had boasted of harboring a fugitive slave in his cellar and writing his sermons with a sword over his ink stand and a pistol in his desk "loaded and ready for defense," denounced Webster in merciless fashion from his pulpit, an attack he would continue even after Webster's death: "No living man has done so much," he cried, "to debauch[12] the conscience of the nation. . . . I know of no deed in American history done by a son of New England to which I can compare this, but the act of Benedict Arnold." "Webster," said Horace Mann, "is a fallen star! Lucifer descending from Heaven!" Longfellow asked the world: "Is it possible? Is this the Titan who hurled mountains at [South Carolina Senator Robert] Hayne years ago?" And Emerson proclaimed that "Every drop of blood in that man's veins has eyes that look downward. . . . Webster's absence of moral faculty is degrading to the country." To William Cullen Bryant, Webster was "a man who has deserted the cause which he lately defended, and deserted it under circumstances which force upon him the imputation of a sordid[13] motive." And to James Russell Lowell he was "the most meanly and foolishly treacherous man I ever heard of."

Charles Sumner, who would be elevated to the Senate upon his departure, enrolled the name of Webster on "the dark list of apostates.[14] Mr. Webster's elaborate treason has done more than anything else to break down the North." Senator William H. Seward, the brilliant "Conscience" Whig [Whig was the name of Webster's political party], called Webster a "traitor to the cause of freedom." A mass meeting in Faneuil Hall condemned the speech as "unworthy of a wise statesman

---

11 **knocked into a cocked hat:** defeated
12 **debauch:** corrupt
13 **sordid:** morally offensive
14 **apostates:** people who have abandoned their faith in a religion or an ideal

and a good man," and resolved that "Constitution or no Constitution, law or no law, we will not allow a fugitive slave to be taken from the state of Massachusetts." As the Massachusetts Legislature enacted further resolutions wholly contrary to the spirit of the Seventh of March speech, one member called Webster "a recreant [disloyal] son of Massachusetts who misrepresents her in the Senate"; and another stated that "Daniel Webster will be a fortunate man if God, in his sparing mercy, shall preserve his life long enough for him to repent of this act and efface[15] this stain on his name."

The Boston *Courier* pronounced that it was "unable to find that any Northern Whig member of Congress concurs with Mr. Webster"; and his old defender, the Boston *Atlas* stated, "His sentiments are not our sentiments nor we venture to say of the Whigs of New England." The New York *Tribune* considered it "unequal to the occasion and unworthy of its author"; the New York *Evening Post* spoke in terms of a "traitorous retreat . . . a man who deserted the cause which he lately defended"; and the Abolitionist press called it "the scarlet infamy of Daniel Webster. . . . An indescribably base and wicked speech." . . .

But he was saddened by the failure of a single other New England Whig to rise to his defense, and he remarked that he was "engaged in a controversy in which I have neither a leader nor a follower from among my own immediate friends. . . . I am tired of standing up here, almost alone from Massachusetts, contending for practical measures absolutely essential to the good of the country. . . . For five months . . . no one of my colleagues manifested the slightest concurrence in my sentiments. . . . Since the 7th of March there has not been an hour in which I have not felt a crushing weight of anxiety. I have sat down to no breakfast or dinner to which I have brought an unconcerned and easy mind."

But, although he sought to explain his objectives and reassure his friends of his continued opposition to slavery, he nevertheless insisted he would "stand on the principle of my speech to the end. . . . If necessary I will take the stump in every village in New England. . . . What is to come of the present commotion in men's minds I cannot foresee; but my own convictions of duty are fixed and strong, and I shall continue to follow those convictions without faltering. . . . In highly excited times it is far easier to fan and feed the flames of discord, than to subdue them; and he who counsels moderation is in danger of being regarded as failing in his duty to his party."

---

15 **efface:** wipe away

Dream in Color

Linda Sánchez, Loretta Sánchez, and Richard Buskin

Loretta Sánchez won her election to the United States House of Representatives in 1996. When her sister, Linda, won her seat six years later, they became the first sisters ever to serve together in the House. Each represents a district in southern California. Together, they wrote a book describing the inner workings of Congress and the challenges of representing their constituents.

Loretta Sánchez

One of the things I learned from our dad early on was that you have to be disciplined, and that you can't always opt for the easy way out. That applied when he signed off on the classes I would take at school. It was always about having a good foundation. "In order to have a good foundation, you must take chemistry." "In order to understand how the world works, you must take physics." "In order to understand what is going on, you must take history." For him, these building blocks would enable you to perform whatever job or opportunity you were given. And so the message was: don't try to go the easy route. Take care of the fundamentals.

Even in the House of Representatives, if you don't understand the basics of a bill, you won't be able to pass it. If you don't understand the rules of the committee or the rules of the House, your opponents will use those rules against you. So, there are some fundamental things you have to learn: how a bill is created, where the power lies, how people can obstruct what you're trying to do. In the beginning, I didn't sit down and read the rules of the committee to figure out how somebody could mess with me, and as a result I often didn't even *know* they were messing with me! However, after being messed with a couple of times I thought, "I'd better go back and read those rules. I'd better know *exactly* what's going on." It's like chess—you have to think ahead. You have to

Linda (left) and Loretta (right) Sánchez began serving together in 2003.

know the moves they can make against you and prepare yourself to counter them.

When I first entered the House and I was on the Military Committee, I had a large Vietnamese population that I represented in my Congressional district. Unlike other committees, the Military handles one big bill for the entire year, dealing with issues such as how many people we're going to have in the military, what we're going to pay them, what kind of health care we're going to provide, how many B2 bombers we're going to buy, and so on. Everything's put in the same bill so I wanted to propose an amendment that would state that the Vietnamese people had fought valiantly[1] alongside us in the Vietnam War. This entailed my making a

---

1   **valiantly:** bravely

hundred copies of the amendment and then explaining it to my colleagues before it went to a vote.

Consisting of just eight sentences, it was really straightforward and basically a no-brainer. Nobody ever challenges you on that sort of thing . . . or so I thought. At that point, I wasn't yet a full member of the House, and there were those who wanted to oust me from the Congress and prevent me from having any success whatsoever. Accordingly, when I proposed the amendment there were immediate groans from the other side. They didn't even want me to read it because it was a no-brainer and everyone wanted to move on. But, after I introduced it, Steve Buyer from Indiana took a point of order—which I didn't even understand at the time—and substituted my amendment with his *own* amendment. This thanked the South Vietnamese, the Australians, the Thais, the South Koreans, the New Zealanders, and the Filipinos, who had been involved in the conflict. So, there it was, a much larger bill that said the same thing as mine, but added all these other nationalities and had *his* name on it.

We debated this for two hours, going back and forth, and when we finally took a vote, I of course lost. Now we had the Buyer substitute amendment, and I was really mad, but what I'd done when I knew I was going to lose was get my staff to prepare another hundred copies of my own amendment, incorporating a change to just one of the sentences. Then, after the vote was in, I turned to Mr. Skelten, the ranking member, and said, "Mr. Skelten, I have another amendment at the desk."

He said, "What would that amendment be about, Miss Sánchez?"

I said, "That amendment would be about recognizing the Vietnamese people in the Vietnam War."

He said, "The amendment being passed out is *different* from the one that was previously offered. Is that correct?"

I said, "Yes, Mr. Skelten, I've changed one of the sentences."

He said, "Thank you."

By now my staff had told me what I had to do to make sure Steve Buyer couldn't substitute. However, before I could say something he tried to raise a point of order. Thankfully, the chairman, Floyd Spence, cut him off. "Is there any discussion on the amendment? If not, I call for the question."

This was a Republican chairman, basically saying "Pipe down and let this lady get her stuff done." It was very kind on his part. I put forward my amendment and they voted yes. But quite frankly, if it hadn't been for the chairman giving me another chance, I wouldn't have been able to get it done. It was all about the pettiness of certain members who were trying to get rid of me, as well as the fairness of Mr. Spence, who could just as easily have said, "We've gone through that, Miss Sánchez. You're not going to introduce that again."

The thing is, had I known the rules, I could have stopped Steve Buyer the first time around. I could have argued the point of order with him, but I didn't know how to do that, and I also didn't understand what he and others were capable of doing. You have to know the basics, you have to be prepared. Constantly. This happens every day. It happens on the House floor, and we always have a member who knows the rules of order. There are a number of them who, when they enter the House, spend hours and hours just sitting there, watching the debate, studying how people raise points of order, and they become experts. So, when you're down there, debating a bill and you're aware that the other side is going to play with you, you must have somebody from your own side who can jump in and know how to stop that. Some members know the rules in and out very, very well, and that's vital. Because no matter what you're doing, you have to know the rules of the game.

Linda Sánchez

When I was first elected to Congress, I could tell that some of the local elected officials at the city level were not confident that I would be an effective member. I mean, I was the age of most of their children, had never held public office, and was in the minority party in Congress. Nevertheless, I took office determined to show them that although I might be young, I was there to do business, and I'd be around for a long time.

Before I even got sworn in, David Obey, the then-ranking member of the Appropriations Committee, called and told me that since some of the appropriations bills from the prior Congress had not been passed, an omnibus appropriations bill—meaning a year-end federal spending package—would be one of the first things that we would vote on after being sworn into Congress. Therefore, he advised me to have some projects ready in the event that they could add them into the omnibus bill.

I represent several small cities that are always strapped for resources. So, taking the bull by the horns, I set up meetings with the city mayors and city managers from each city. At each meeting, I would ask the mayor and city manager about their priorities for their city in the upcoming year, and I would also ask them how I could help at the federal level. In many instances, I told them there would be federal funding opportunities as the appropriations process got underway.

Serving in Congress requires balancing one's interests with those of others in order to reach agreements on policies.

One of the smaller cities I represent desperately needed funding to renovate and repave its major street, which was old and falling into disrepair. For ten years the city had been begging its former congressman to try to help it get federal funds for the roadwork, but he had never secured any real funding for the project. Well, when the time came, and Mr. Obey asked for projects, that was one of the projects I submitted. It made it into the omnibus bill, and the omnibus bill passed. That meant that after being in Congress for only six weeks, I was able to tell this city that I had gotten it the funding! And whereas before the city had been skeptical, I now had a victory to show them, and it was grateful.

Suddenly, people sat up and took notice. Here I was, a freshman in the minority, and I was producing for my constituents. Of course, none of this would have been possible if Mr. Obey had not been looking out for the freshmen and gone out of his way to help us, so for that I will always be grateful to him. But the other lesson that I learned was that because I took the time to meet with each city's leadership and listen to their needs, I was prepared to move quickly when the time came.

Every year, before the appropriations process begins, I schedule these meetings, and the cities I represent appreciate them tremendously. As a result, I have seen city leader's attitudes about me change for the better. After two terms, I began getting endorsements from Republican city council members who have basically told me they may not agree with my positions on some issues, but I look out for, and take care of, my cities and they appreciate that. Proving I care and can deliver are things that, hopefully, constituents will value, and therefore convince them to keep me around for a long time. . . .

Sometimes you have to sacrifice the short-term strategy for the long-term strategy. It's not a sprint, it's a marathon. So, although you may not be running your fastest time in the first mile, if you're tenacious and you're determined and you're moving at a good clip, eventually you're going to win that race, because you'll have the energy to persevere throughout the twenty-six miles. That's the same with many things in life—it's about the marathon, not sprinting, and you don't want to start out full speed ahead, because that way you'll crash and burn. It's the long game, and you have to look at it in that perspective. We didn't get where we wanted in mile one, but we're going to get there eventually. And if it takes a little bit longer, then we're going to need a little more patience.

Number of Women in Congress

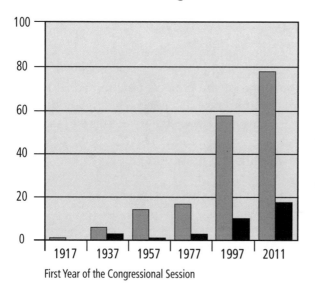

First Year of the Congressional Session

Loretta and Linda Sánchez followed in the path of Representative Jeannette Rankin, who was the first woman elected to Congress. Rankin, a Montana Republican, took office in 1917. In a 2011 survey of the percentage of women in national legislatures, the United States ranked near the middle.

Number of women in the House of Representatives
Number of women in the Senate

Source: Website of the United States House of Representatives

LIFE IN THE SENATE

STEPHEN L. CARTER

*The Senate might be the world's most exclusive club. It is small—only
100 members. Its members are elite—almost all are well educated and
wealthy. It is very difficult to get into—candidates spend tens of
millions of dollars to gain admission. The members of this club have
the difficult job of representing everyone in their state. Stephen L.
Carter takes a look at how senators conduct themselves.*

A few years ago, a friend asked me over lunch whether I knew of any
"dirt"—his word—on a person who had recently been nominated to a
post requiring Senate confirmation. The "groups," he said, had decided
to oppose the appointment, and were trolling[1] for information. In other
words, a smear campaign was coming.

This tale comes to mind after economist Peter Diamond's dramatic
and angry withdrawal of his candidacy for a post on the Board of
Governors of the Federal Reserve, and the looming battle over the
nomination of John Bryson to serve as Secretary of Commerce.

Diamond, who last year was awarded the Nobel Memorial Prize in
Economic Science, was opposed by Republicans led by Senator Richard
Shelby of Alabama. Although Shelby claimed this was because Diamond
had too little experience and that he couldn't back "monetary policy
decisions made by board members who are learning on the job," the real
aim was to turn his confirmation process into a referendum on President
Barack Obama's economic policies.

In Bryson's case, it isn't his expertise that is under fire—he ran a
giant California utility, Edison International (EIX)—but his role as a
co-founder of the Natural Resources Defense Council,[2] which has stirred
opposition even among some Democrats. Senate Republicans have
promised not to allow a vote on the nomination until Obama submits for

---

1 **trolling:** searching
2 **Natural Resources Defense Council:** a large and influential environmental organization

congressional approval the pending free-trade agreements with Panama, Colombia, and South Korea.

Unfair and Traditional

None of this is particularly fair to Diamond or Bryson. Still, the clamor of outrage among their supporters is, to say the least, ahistorical. What is happening today is no different from what has happened to nominees over the past half century or so. Or what has happened, at least, when politicians and interest groups have spotted opportunities to use a confirmation fight for political advantage.

We are so accustomed to vicious and distorted attacks on nominees for judicial office that we might easily forget that others, too, can find themselves caught up in unexpected and nasty tussles. One need only recall the treatment of Lani Guinier, President Bill Clinton's initial nominee to lead the Civil Rights Division of the Justice Department, whose opponents distorted her scholarship beyond recognition.

The Gates Case

Or consider Robert Gates, the outgoing Secretary of Defense. He was selected by President Ronald Reagan to run the Central Intelligence Agency in 1987, but the nomination was withdrawn when Democrats protested his alleged involvement in the Iran-Contra scandal.[3] (The actual accusation was that Gates had known more about the affair than he told investigators, but the independent counsel wound up not pursuing the matter, and Gates finally got the job in the administration of George H.W. Bush.)

And, speaking of the CIA, one might also recall Theodore Sorensen, who was nominated in 1977 to head the agency but withdrew his nomination after accusations that he was a pacifist. Indeed, although only a handful of executive branch nominations are actually defeated, the number generating controversy rises steadily.

Democrats think only Republicans behave this way, and Republicans think the same about Democrats. The truth is, everybody does it, and with increasing frequency. Diamond was the 20th of Obama's executive branch nominations to have been withdrawn.

---

3 **Iran-Contra scandal:** a scandal in the 1980s in which the Reagan administration illegally sold weapons to Iran in an attempt to free Americans held hostage there and to illegally fund a rebel movement in Nicaragua known as the Contras

Opportunities to Communicate

Political scientists suggest that senators use high-profile nomination battles as opportunities to communicate their own views to their constituents and to the interest groups so necessary to election. Now that the Internet has made organizing easier and has coupled elected officials more tightly to the interest groups that monitor their every word, the number of nominations that generate controversy is bound to increase.

Battles over confirmations are often fierce. Some result in compromise–and some do not.

One reason the attacks on nominees are so strident[4] is to overcome the presumption that the president is entitled to "his own team." But that presumption is a myth. The Founders envisioned a heavy Senate role in appointments. Alexander Hamilton suggested in *The Federalist* that the requirement of confirmation would, among other things, keep the president from filling the executive branch with those who were "in some way or other personally allied to him."

Complexity Added Animosity[5]

Indeed, one reason that there were scarcely any squabbles over cabinet members for the first 90 years of the republic is that the presidents consulted closely with leading senators in deciding whom to appoint.

The tradition began to decline as governing grew more complex, and was thrown over entirely during the presidency of Rutherford B. Hayes[6] (1877–1881). Part of the problem was that executive appointments had become part of the spoils system[7] for powerful senators. But, as so often, we tossed out the baby with the bath water. Determined to end the corruption, Hayes forced his appointments down the Senate's collective

---

4   **strident:** loud with an angry tone

5   **animosity:** dislike or hatred

6   **Rutherford B. Hayes:** Hayes was elected president only after agreeing to remove Northern troops from the South, where they had been protecting the rights of ex-slaves since the end of the Civil War in 1865

7   **spoils system:** the practice of appointing one's political supporters to government office

throat. Thus Hayes, known to history for the infamous bargain that bought the presidency at the cost of ending Reconstruction, also largely subdued the Senate as a serious partner in the appointments process.

Since that time, presidents have worked hard to keep their executive appointments away from serious Senate scrutiny. One way to do that is to make recess appointments, intended by the Founders to tide the nation over when the Senate happens not to be in session. Nowadays, presidents use this dodge[8] to get people into slots the Senate might not let them have. Obama has made almost 30 recess appointments in his first two years in office, not an unusually high number—unless your baseline is the way the constitutional system of checks and balances is supposed to work.

Yielding to Temptation

Given the ever-greater likelihood that executive branch and agency nominees will run into trouble, it is easy to see why presidents yield to the temptation to thwart[9] the system: They know Congress will never punish them for it.

The confirmation process may not be fixable. In the nation's early days, the Senate had to approve fewer than a dozen of the president's aides. Today, more than 500 executive branch posts require Senate confirmation. With politicians, interest groups, journalists and bloggers engaged in the constant quest for advantage, some nominees will always become objects of controversy. There are too many contested issues, too many flashpoints,[10] and—most important—too many constituencies demanding constant signals that their particular concerns are uppermost in the minds of their elected officials.

Many reforms have been suggested. Congress is considering a significant reduction in the number of positions requiring confirmation, an increased centralization of power in the executive that would have appalled the Founders and should appall us, too.

A Shrinking Solution

A rarely mentioned possibility is to shrink by a significant amount the size and scope of the federal government. A smaller executive branch

---

8 **dodge:** the act of avoiding something
9 **thwart:** prevent or oppose
10 **flashpoints:** the points at which an important change takes place

SOUTHERN CHIVALRY — ARGUMENT versus CLUB'S.

One of the worst moments in the history of the United States Congress occurred in the Senate on May 22, 1856. Representative Preston Brooks severely beat Senator Charles Sumner. The senator had made a speech in which he ridiculed Brooks' uncle for his views on slavery.

would mean less need for Senate confirmation. Indeed, the steady rise of confirmation fights in the years after World War II predictably tracks the steady rise of federal agencies. Yet significant shrinkage seems politically unlikely—every agency lives symbiotically[11] with several well-organized interest groups.

Yes, it would be lovely if grasping interest groups would stop digging for dirt and hungry politicians would stop grandstanding, but democracy is rarely lovely. Democracy is clamorous[12] and disputatious.[13] The more distant people feel from those who govern them, the louder their clamor to be heard. The clamor doesn't necessarily lead to right answers or wise decisions; but democracy is mostly process, not result.

Those loud voices—those out-of-context sound bites, those sudden savagings of the reputations of the innocent—have always been part of our democracy. It is ugly and painful and often unfair to the innocent. It is also the American way; and with a federal government so vast, and interest groups so diverse, and the battle for news coverage so intense, it is likely to get worse.

---

11 **symbiotically:** describing a relationship that benefits both people or things
12 **clamorous:** loud
13 **disputatious:** filled with arguments

CITIZENS AS POWERFUL LOBBYISTS

LEE HAMILTON

According to the Constitution, members of Congress get their power from representing the people of the country. Yet, polls indicate that many Americans feel that Congress does not represent them very well. They believe that Congress pays more attention to lobbyists, people who are employed to influence legislators, than to ordinary citizens. The author of this article, Lee Hamilton, served an Indiana district in the House of Representatives for thirty-four years. Here, he explains why he thinks citizens are effective lobbyists.

There has been much worrisome news lately concerning the lobbying industry.

Revelations about the string-pulling of super-lobbyist Jack Abramoff[1] have pulled aside a veil that many Washington players wish had remained in place. The upcoming start of the new Medicare drug subsidy[2] has unleashed a health-care industry feeding frenzy, as various interests try to affect to their advantage how the regulations get written and carried out.

It is all enough to make an ordinary citizen think that the choicest fruits of our democracy are available only to those who can afford to hire people to harvest them.

So it might seem a strange time to suggest that you and your neighbors share some significant advantages when it comes to affecting the course of events in Washington. Yet it's true.

The lobbying industry may have a leg up in some respects—money, contacts, professional smarts, and a seemingly endless supply of Super Bowl tickets and posh[3] restaurant reservations among them—but these

---

1 **Jack Abramoff:** one of the most powerful lobbyists before being convicted of mail fraud and conspiracy in 2006
2 **Medicare drug subsidy:** a federal health care program for the elderly that in 2006 began to subsidize the cost of prescription drugs
3 **posh:** fashionable, luxurious

are not the only things that count. In fact, they can be outweighed by ordinary citizens who are resolved to make the most of their own, simple strengths.

First among these is the fact that you are represented in Washington by a House member and two senators. In my experience, most members of Congress take very seriously their role in representing the needs and desires of constituents back home. Not only does this mean that you can get a foot in the door, it also means that—assuming they want to be re-elected—your representatives will be reluctant to ignore you. You start out with access that most lobbyists have to work to gain.

Beyond this basic constitutional fact, members of Congress also know that the folks back home are often in a good position to understand how a piece of legislation might affect them. They are ready to listen. So when your congressman comes home, it gives you an opportunity to meet in an informal way—over a cup of coffee, for instance—that most lobbyists can only envy.

Moreover, because members of Congress know they need to gauge the sentiments of the communities they represent, you and your neighbors possess a distinct advantage over well-funded lobbyists: If you speak directly and forcefully about how a bill might affect you and your family, you have a kind of credibility that lobbyists simply cannot match.

Most Effective Means of Citizen Advocacy

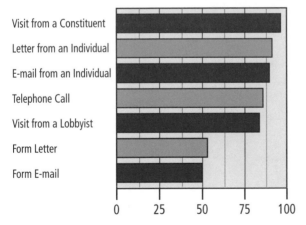

A poll of congressional staff members rated the effectiveness of different methods used by citizens to influence members of Congress. The most effective methods received the highest ratings.

Source: Perceptions of Citizen Advocacy on Capitol Hill, Congressional Management Foundation (October to December 2010). www.CongressFoundation.org.

And because you live in your community, not in Washington, you have direct access to other players that no member of Congress can ignore. You can appeal to your local media—which most members of Congress consider more important than the national media. And you also have the chance to join or form coalitions with groups in your area to oppose or support legislation, and even to work for or against your representative in Congress.

Finally, you have a home-turf advantage. Most lobbyists live in or around Washington and come from places all over the United States—indeed, from all over the world. You, on the other hand, come from the same region as your House member and the same state as your senators. You have experiences, culture, slang, even friends and acquaintances in common.

This puts you a step ahead in what may be the single most important task for any lobbyist, professional or citizen: establishing a good ongoing relationship with a member of Congress. You may not always agree with one another, but if your representative knows that you have valuable insights from your local perspective or constructive arguments to add to what he or she is hearing from others, that goes a long way toward leveling the playing field.

One of the most successful lobbying efforts by citizens in American history was the civil rights movement of the 1950s and and 1960s.

I don't want to play down the influence that professional lobbyists enjoy. There are many thousands of them now, and most of them do their work with skill and diligence. But for an ordinary citizen who has something to say, this should be at worst a challenge, not a barrier. The deck is stacked against you only as long as you allow it to be.

America's Most Notorious Lobbyist

Leslie Stahl

The First Amendment protects the rights of citizens to petition Congress and attempt to influence the decisions it makes. Lobbyists are people who do this professionally. Critics charge that lobbyists have too much power—that members of Congress listen more to lobbyists who work for particular interests than to the voters. Jack Abramoff was once one of the most effective and highly paid lobbyists in Washington, D.C. His clients included Indian tribes, foreign countries, toy manufacturers, and educational organizations. However, in 2006 he was convicted of mail fraud and conspiracy for actions connected to lobbying. He spent over three years in jail. The following excerpt is from a television interview between Abramoff and journalist Leslie Stahl after he was released. He begins by responding to the charge that lobbyists "buy," or control, members of Congress.

Abramoff: First, I think most congressmen don't feel they're being bought. Most congressmen, I think, can in their own mind justify the system.

Stahl: Rationalize[1]

Abramoff:—rationalize it and, by the way, we wanted as lobbyists for them to feel that way.

Stahl (to audience): Abramoff would provide freebies[2] and gifts—looking for favors for his clients in return. He'd lavish[3] certain congressmen and senators with access to private jets and junkets[4] to the world's great golf destinations like St. Andrews in Scotland. Free meals at his own upscale Washington restaurant and access to the best tickets to all the area's sporting events; including two skyboxes at Washington Redskins games.

---

1 **rationalize:** to explain in a way that denies responsibility
2 **freebies:** items or services given without charge
3 **lavish:** to give extravagantly
4 **junkets:** trips paid for another person

Abramoff: I spent over a million dollars a year on tickets to sporting events and concerts and what not at all the venues.

Stahl: A million dollars?

Abramoff: Ya. Ya.

Stahl: For the best seats?

Abramoff: The best seats. I had two people on my staff whose virtual full-time job was booking tickets. We were Ticketmaster for these guys.

How does the artist make the dome of the Capitol look like the head of a fish? Explain the symbolism used in this image.

Stahl: And the congressman or senator could take his favorite people from his district to the game—

Abramoff: The congressman or senator uh, could take two dozen of his favorite people from their district.

Stahl: Was all that legal?

Abramoff: We would certainly try to make the activity legal, if we could. At times we didn't care.

Stahl (to audience): But the "best way" to get a congressional office to do his bidding—he says—was to offer a staffer a job that could triple his salary.

Abramoff: When we would become friendly with an office and they were important to us, and the chief of staff was a competent person, I would say or my staff would say to him or her at some point, "You know, when you're done working on the Hill,[5] we'd very much like you to consider coming to work for us." Now the moment I said that to them or any of our staff said that to 'em, that was it. We owned them. And what does that mean? Every request from our office, every request of our clients, everything that we want, they're gonna do. And not only that, they're gonna think of things we can't think of to do.

---

5 **Hill:** an informal term for Congress, short for Capitol Hill

[The scene changes to another interview.]

Neil Volz: Jack Abramoff could sweet talk a dog off a meat truck, that's how persuasive he was.

Stahl (to audience): Neil Volz was one of the staffers Abramoff was talking about. He was chief of staff to Congressman Bob Ney, who as chairman of the House Administration Committee had considerable power to dispense[6] favors. Abramoff targeted Volz and offered him a job.

Stahl: You're the chief of staff of a powerful congressman. And Jack owns you and you haven't even left working for the congressman.

Volz: I have the distinct memory of, you know, negotiating with Jack at a hockey game. So we're, you know, just a few rows back. The crowd's goin' crazy. And Jack and I are havin' a business conversation. And, you know, I'm—I'm wrestlin' with how much I think I should get paid. And then five minutes later we're—he's askin' me questions about some clients of his.

Stahl: When you look back was that the corrupting moment?

Volz: I think we were guilty of engaging in a corrupt relationship. So there were several corrupting moments. There isn't just one moment. There were many.

Abramoff: At the end of the day most of the people that I encountered who worked on Capitol Hill wanted to come work on K Street,[7] wanted to be lobbyists.

Stahl: You're telling me this, the genius of figuring out you could own the office by offering a job to the chief of staff, say. I'm having two reactions. One is brilliant. And the other is I'm sick to my stomach.

Abramoff: Right. Evil. Yeah. Terrible.

Stahl: 'Cause it's hurting our country.

Abramoff: Shameful. Absolutely. It's the worst thing that could happen. All parts of the system.

Stahl: I'm mad at you.

Abramoff: I was mad at me—

Stahl: I'm not kidding. I'm not kidding.

Abramoff: Look I did things and I was involved in the system I should not have been in. I'm ashamed of the fact I was there, the very

---

6 **dispense:** to give
7 **K Street:** a street in Washington, D.C., where many lobbyists have offices

reason why now I'm speaking about it. And now I'm trying to do something, in recompense,[8] is the fact that I thought it was—it was wrong of me to do it. . . .

Stahl (to audience): Abramoff prided himself on being a man who did good. He was devoutly religious and exorbitantly[9] charitable and he says he gave away 80 percent of his earnings. When he fell from grace, his reputation was in tatters[10] because it was not just that he had corrupted Congress—it was found he had cheated his clients, like the Indian tribes.

Abramoff: Most of the money I made I gave away, to either communal or charitable causes. So I thought frankly I was one of the most moral lobbyists out there. . . .

Stahl: I really think what you were doing was—was subverting[11] the essence of our system.

Abramoff: Yes. Absolutely right. But our system is flawed and has to be fixed. Human beings populate our system. Human beings are weak.

Stahl: And you preyed on that?

Abramoff: I did. I was one of many who did. I did. And I'm ashamed of that fact.

Stahl (to audience): He was sent to a medium security facility in Cumberland, Maryland. When he was released last June, he began working as an accountant at a kosher[12] pizza parlor. Turns out Jack Abramoff was broke, partly because he is paying off nearly $24 million in restitution[13] to the Indian tribes. Today he lives in his old house in Maryland with his wife, five children and the two doberman pinschers Mrs. Abramoff bought to protect the family while he was away. . . .

He says the most important thing that needs to be done is to prohibit members of Congress and their staff from ever becoming lobbyists in Washington.

Abramoff: If you make the choice to serve the public, public service, then serve the public, not yourself. When you're done, go home. Washington's a dangerous place. Don't hang around.

---

8 **recompense:** payment to make up for causing damage
9 **exorbitantly:** excessively
10 **tatters:** shreds
11 **subverting:** destroying completely
12 **kosher:** following Jewish dietary laws
13 **restitution:** the act of paying for damage one caused

American People Hire Lobbyist

THE ONION

According to the Constitution, every citizen is represented in Congress by one representative and two senators. In addition, since nearly every industry, large nonprofit organization, and religious body employs lobbyists, most citizens are represented by several people trying to influence Congress. The Onion, a satirical newspaper, humorously suggests this is not enough.

WASHINGTON—Citing a desire to gain influence in Washington, the American people confirmed Friday that they have hired high-powered D.C. lobbyist Jack Weldon of the firm Patton Boggs to help advance their agenda in Congress.

Known among Beltway[1] insiders for his ability to sway public policy on behalf of massive corporations such as Johnson & Johnson, Monsanto, and AT&T, Weldon, 53, is expected to use his vast network of political connections to give his new client a voice in the legislative process.

Weldon is reportedly charging the American people $795 an hour.

"Unlike R.J. Reynolds, Pfizer, or Bank of America, the U.S. populace[2] lacks the access to public officials required to further its legislative goals," a statement from the nation read in part. "Jack Weldon gives us that access."

"His daily presence in the Capitol will ensure the American people finally get a seat at the table," the statement continued. "And it will allow him to advance our message that everyone, including Americans, deserves to be represented in Washington."

The 310-million-member group said it will rely on Weldon's considerable clout to ensure its concerns are taken into account when Congress addresses issues such as education, immigration, national

---

1 **Beltway:** a nickname for the government in Washington, D.C.; it refers to Interstate 495, a highway that completely circles Washington, D.C., and is known as the Capital Beltway
2 **populace:** the typical people

security, health care, transportation, the economy, affordable college tuition, infrastructure, jobs, equal rights, taxes, Social Security, the environment, housing, the national debt, agriculture, energy, alternative energy, nutrition, imports, exports, foreign relations, the arts, and crime.

Sources confirmed that Weldon is already scheduled to have drinks Monday with several members of the Senate Appropriations Committee to discuss saving the middle class.

"If you have a problem, say, with America's atrocious[3] treatment of its veterans, you can't just pick up a phone and call your local congressman," Weldon told reporters from his office on K Street[4] Monday. "You need someone on the inside who understands how democracy works; someone who knows how to grease the wheels a little."

Weldon said that after successfully advocating on behalf of Goldman Sachs and BP, he is relishing the opportunity to lobby for the American people, calling it the "challenge of a lifetime." The veteran D.C. power player admitted that his new client is at a disadvantage because it lacks the money and power of other groups.

"The goal is to make it seem politically advantageous for legislators to keep the American people in mind when making laws," Weldon said. "Lawmakers are going to ask me, 'Why should I care about the American people? What's in it for me?' And it will be up to me and my team to find some reason why they should consider putting poverty and medical care for children on the legislative docket."[5]

"To be honest," Weldon added, "the American people have always been perceived as a little naive[6] when it comes to their representative government. But having me on their side sends a clear message that they're finally serious and want to play ball."

According to Washington heavyweights, hiring Weldon is an immediate game changer and should force politicians to take citizens' concerns seriously for the first time in decades. Moreover, sources said, Weldon will be able to help lawmakers see the American people as more than just a low-priority fringe group.

"Jack is very good at what he does," said Joseph Pearlman, a

---

3   **atrocious:** terrible or cruel
4   **K Street:** a street in Washington, D.C., where many lobbyists have offices
5   **docket:** agenda
6   **naive:** lacking understanding about the world

headhunter for the McCormick Group who specializes in placing lobbyists. "He can take an issue that is nowhere on the congressional radar, like the pursuit of happiness, for example, and make it politically relevant. The next time Congress passes a bill dealing with civil rights or taxes, I wouldn't be surprised if the U.S. populace is mentioned somewhere in the final language."

Though Weldon has only been on the job for three days, legislators have already seemed to take notice.

"Before today, I'd actually never heard of this group," Rep. Eric Cantor (R-VA) told reporters. "But if Jack says they're worth my time, I'll take a look and see if maybe there are some areas where our interests overlap."

"But I'm not making any promises," he added. "I'm a very busy man."

What can you infer is the cartoonist's attitude toward the 14,000 lobbyists who are employed in Washington, D.C.?

"American People Hire Lobbyist" from *The Onion*. Reprinted with permission of THE ONION. Copyright © 2011, by ONION, INC. www.theonion.com.

Responding to Cluster One

How Well Does Congress Represent the People?
Critical Thinking Skill INFERRING INFORMATION

1. What can you infer about John F. Kennedy's view of Daniel Webster's decision to support the Compromise of 1850? Use the following chart to show how Kennedy's choice of details reveals his point of view.

Kennedy's Point of View:	
Detail	**Analysis of Detail**

2. Based on the experience of Linda and Loretta Sánchez, what can you infer about the skills that a member of Congress needs to represent constituents well?

3. What solution does Stephen L. Carter see in the appointment and confirmation approach? What can you infer about his point of view toward the powers of Congress and the president? Support your answers with specific details from the text.

4. Based on the selection by Lee Hamilton, what can you infer he would say about the information in the graph on page 39?

5. Summarize what you can infer about Jack Abramoff's view of Washington, D.C., from his concluding comment that "Washington's a dangerous place."

6. What can you infer is the main idea of "American People Hire Lobbyist"? Cite specific examples of irony in your answer.

Writing Activity: Infer Information and Write an Argument

Do members of Congress have a greater responsibility to their constituents or to their own convictions? Find comments from members of Congress from which you can infer how they view their responsibility. Write an essay in which you use these inferences in an argument supporting your point of view on this question.

A Strong Argument

- makes a clear claim

- supports the claim with logical reasons and relevant evidence

- uses transitional words and phrases to link major ideas

CLUSTER TWO

WHAT MAKES A PRESIDENT GREAT?
Critical Thinking Skill EVALUATING ARGUMENTS

As He Shall Judge Necessary

Akhil Reed Amar

When George Washington took office as the first president, no one knew how to address him. Some wanted "Your Excellency" or "Your Serene Highness." Washington asked a friend if "High Mightiness" might work. Finally, people settled on simply "Mr. President." The debate over a title reflected a deeper question: What powers should a president have? Constitutional scholar Akhil Reed Amar considers how some of the writers of the Constitution viewed the office.

Article II concluded its roster of specific presidential powers and duties with language authorizing the chief executive to inform Congress periodically of the state of the union and recommend any measures he judged fitting; to convene Congress in emergencies; to receive foreign diplomats; to "take Care that the Laws be faithfully executed"; and to commission all executive and judicial officers. This catalogue of responsibilities envisioned the president as a generalist focused on the big picture. While Congress would enact statutes and courts would decide cases one at a time, the president would oversee the enforcement of *all* the laws at once—a sweeping mandate[1] that invited him to ponder legal patterns in the largest sense and inevitably conferred some discretion on him in defining his enforcement philosophy and priorities. So, too, the president's responsibility to mull[2] the state of the union as a whole and to offer any recommendation that he should "judge necessary and expedient" underscored the breadth of his mandate as the one constitutional officer always in session and presiding over the whole nation.

Ambassadors might arrive at any time, and the president would be there to receive them. Crises might arise at any moment, and the president would be there to decide whether and when to convene

---

1 **mandate:** declaration giving authority
2 **mull:** think about

The Ten Top-Ranked Presidents	
1.	Franklin Roosevelt (1933 to 1945)
2.	Theodore Roosevelt (1901 to 1909)
3.	Abraham Lincoln (1861 to 1865)
4.	George Washington (1789 to 1797)
5.	Thomas Jefferson (1801 to 1809)
6.	James Madison (1809 to 1817)
7.	James Monroe (1817 to 1825)
8.	Woodrow Wilson (1913 to 1921)
9.	Harry Truman (1945 to 1953)
10.	Dwight Eisenhower (1953 to 1961)

These rankings were based on a survey of 238 presidential scholars. Each president's term in office is listed in parentheses.

Source: Siena College Research Institute Presidential Ranking Survey. Survey conducted in 2010.

Congress, though he would have no British-style royal power to dissolve or prorogue[3] Congress. Military and civil vacancies would occur around the clock, and the president would be there to superintend the process of commissioning replacements.

Beyond a president's macro-discretion in setting general priorities, many individual statutes were expected to contain significant zones of micro discretion. Filling in these gaps was a classic executive function, as was the related fact-finding power to determine whether certain statutory conditions had actually been met. Thus, if Congress legislated that in the event of situation X, legal consequence Y should follow, congressmen themselves would as a rule not be the judges of whether X had in fact occurred. Rather, the executive branch would typically make a determination in the first instance, subject to judicial oversight whose precise scope might vary widely, depending on the issue.

Despite its elaborate gestures toward specificity and enumeration, Article II left much to be filled in by practice. To clarify that America's chief executive would be much less than an English king and much more than a typical state governor was to say something important, but a vast space separated these two poles. Key questions remained: Just how far did the commander-in-chief power extend? How broadly should the presidential power to receive ambassadors he construed? Was the president's responsibility to "take Care that the Laws be faithfully executed" a narrow ministerial duty or a sweeping font of power?

---

3   **prorogue:** to end a meeting of a body

Granted that the residuum[4] of "executive Power" in the opening words of Article II surely encompassed Lincoln's mandate to save the Union and Washington's authority to control his executive-branch deputies, what else fell within the residuum?

The evident openness of the text here reflected the framers' genuine uncertainty as they struggled to invent a wholly new sort of executive. Thanks to its gaps and silences, Article II in effect delegated authority to the political branches to negotiate more concrete settlements. Doubtless most Founders looked forward to the leadership of George Washington and expected him to transform a sparse text into actual institutional practice and precedent. Hence the special authority of the settlements and understandings reached during the Washington Administration.

What Article II did make emphatically clear from start to finish was that the president would be personally responsible for his branch. Though he would be aided by subordinates in discharging his many and varied functions, the Constitution took pains to disavow the idea of a collective cabinet or directory behind whom he might hide. In the appointments context, the document pointedly repudiated the New York experiment, which united the governor and a number of senators into a council that made appointments by a collective and opaque vote. According to Hamilton/Publius in *The Federalist* No. 70, the New York council had resulted in "scandalous appointments to important offices," but when the public made inquiries, it was almost impossible to apportion blame as individual council members pointed fingers at one another. Following Massachusetts rather than New York, Article II required the president alone to openly nominate his candidates, enabling the public to assess the nominator while the Senate assessed the nominees.

As *The Federalist* No. 70 observed in language distilling earlier statements by Wilson, Madison, Ellsworth, Gouverneur Morris, Charles Pinckney, and others, Article II was structured to prevent a president from claiming, "I was overruled by my council." Unlike state executive councils, a president's cabinet would be composed of men that he himself had nominated, or at least men that he had not removed. In clear contrast to its rules requiring a president to woo the Senate in his nominations and treaties, nowhere did Article II oblige him to seek his executive subordinates' advice, much less their consent. As Iredell

---

4 **residuum:** remainder

explained in urging ratification: "The President will personally have the credit of good, or the censure of bad measures; since, though he may ask advice, he is to use his own judgment in following or rejecting it." The Article II opinions clause invited a president to seek a cabinet officer's opinion only on issues within that officer's "respective" executive department but said nothing to encourage a president to poll his cabinet as a group.

Early presidential practice nevertheless drifted somewhat toward a collective cabinet, yielding to the gravitational pull of widespread state executive-branch practice. Yet even as weak presidents occasionally tried to duck behind strong cabinets, Article II fixed the public eye on the chief executive himself. Legend tells us that Lincoln once submitted a pet proposal to his cabinet and, when met with a unanimous chorus of nays, quipped that "the aye has it." Though too good to be true, the legend captures a deep truth about Article II. James Wilson framed the issue well in 1791:

"The British throne is surrounded by counsellors. With regard to their authority, a profound and mysterious silence is observed. . . . Between power and responsibility, they interpose an impenetrable barrier. . . . Amidst [the ministers'] multitude, and the secrecy, with which business, especially that of a perilous kind, is transacted, it will be often difficult to select the culprits; still more so, to punish them. . . . In the United States, our first executive magistrate is not obnubilated[5] behind the mysterious obscurity of counsellors. Power is communicated to him with liberality, though with ascertained limitations. To him the provident[6] or improvident use of it is to be ascribed.[7] For the first, he will have and deserve undivided applause. For the last, he will be subject to censure;[8] if necessary, to punishment. He is the dignified, but accountable magistrate of a free and great people."

---

5 **obnubilated:** hidden
6 **provident:** sensible
7 **ascribed:** attributed to
8 **censure:** criticism

GREAT PRESIDENTIAL SPEECHES

As public figures, presidents provide leadership, inspiration, focus, and comfort to the American public through their speeches. The following speeches or excerpts from speeches are among the most famous and influential addresses by presidents.

George Washington: The Farewell Address

After George Washington died in 1799, Henry Lee of Virginia commented that Washington was "first in war, first in peace, and first in the hearts of his countrymen." Today, we could add that Washington remains first, or nearly first, in polls asking historians to choose the most effective presidents. As the first president, everything George Washington did made him a leader. He set a pattern for other presidents to follow—or break away from. In his final major speech as president, known as The Farewell Address, Washington summarized the principles that had guided him in dealing with other countries. These comments shaped the foreign policy of the United States for many generations.

The great rule of conduct for us in regard to foreign nations is in extending our commercial relations, to have with them as little political connection as possible. So far as we have already formed engagements, let them be fulfilled with perfect good faith. Here let us stop. Europe has a set of primary interests which to us have none; or a very remote relation. Hence she must be engaged in frequent controversies, the causes of which are essentially foreign to our concerns. Hence, therefore, it must be unwise in us to implicate ourselves by artificial ties in the ordinary vicissitudes[1] of her politics, or the ordinary combinations and collisions of her friendships or enmities.

Our detached and distant situation invites and enables us to pursue a different course. If we remain one people under an efficient government, the period is not far off when we may defy material injury from external annoyance; when we may take such an attitude as will cause the

---

1 **vicissitudes:** changes, often sudden and unexpected

neutrality we may at any time resolve upon to be scrupulously respected; when belligerent nations, under the impossibility of making acquisitions upon us, will not lightly hazard the giving us provocation; when we may choose peace or war, as our interest, guided by justice, shall counsel.

Why forego the advantages of so peculiar a situation? Why quit our own to stand upon foreign ground? Why, by interweaving our destiny with that of any part of Europe, entangle our peace and prosperity in the toils of European ambition, rivalship, interest, humor, or caprice?[2]

It is our true policy to steer clear of permanent alliances with any portion of the foreign world; so far, I mean, as we are now at liberty to do it; for let me not be understood as capable of patronizing infidelity[3] to existing engagements. I hold the maxim no less applicable to public than to private affairs, that honesty is always the best policy. I repeat it, therefore, let those engagements be observed in their genuine sense. But, in my opinion, it is unnecessary and would be unwise to extend them.

GEORGE WASHINGTON 1840 Horatio Greenough

The sculptor wanted to honor Washington by showing him in the style used by artists in classical Greece two thousand years earlier. However, his work shocked many Americans when it was created because it shows Washington without a shirt.

---

2 **caprice:** a quick change of mind
3 **infidelity:** lack of trustworthiness

Abraham Lincoln: The Gettysburg Address

On November 19, 1863, the United States was in the midst of the Civil War. On that day, President Abraham Lincoln gave a short speech at the dedication of a military cemetery at Gettysburg, Pennsylvania. He expressed his vision for the country. His words received little attention at the time. However, about a decade later, people began to view the speech with greater respect. Three decades later, the speech was considered a masterpiece. Today, it is probably the best-known and most highly regarded speech by any American president.

Four score[4] and seven years ago our fathers brought forth on this continent a new nation, conceived in liberty, and dedicated to the proposition that all men are created equal.

Now we are engaged in a great civil war, testing whether that nation, or any nation, so conceived and so dedicated, can long endure. We are met on a great battlefield of that war. We have come to dedicate a portion of that field, as a final resting place for those who here gave their lives that that nation might live. It is altogether fitting and proper that we should do this.

But, in a larger sense, we cannot dedicate, we cannot consecrate,[5] we cannot hallow this ground. The brave men, living and dead, who struggled here, have consecrated it, far above our poor power to add or detract. The world will little note, nor long remember what we say here, but it can never forget what they did here. It is for us the living, rather, to be

ABRAHAM LINCOLN 1869 George Peter Alexander Healy

What traits of Lincoln does this painting show?

---

4 **score:** twenty

5 **consecrate:** dedicate or make sacred

dedicated here to the unfinished work which they who fought here have thus far so nobly advanced. It is rather for us to be here dedicated to the great task remaining before us—that from these honored dead we take increased devotion to that cause for which they gave the last full measure of devotion—that we here highly resolve that these dead shall not have died in vain—that this nation, under God, shall have a new birth of freedom—and that government of the people, by the people, for the people, shall not perish from the earth.

Franklin Roosevelt: The State of the Union, 1941

The Constitution requires the president to regularly communicate with Congress about the "state of the Union." Out of this requirement developed the tradition that the president gives a major speech each January summarizing the conditions in the country and laying out the administration's agenda for the coming year. One of the most memorable State of the Union addresses was delivered by Franklin Roosevelt on January 6, 1941. He spoke to a nervous nation. At home, the United States was slowly pulling out of the deepest economic depression in its history. Overseas, World War II was already raging in Europe and eastern Asia. People wondered if the United States would soon be at war. They looked to the president to explain the world situation.

Mr. President, Mr. Speaker, Members of the Seventy-seventh Congress:

I address you, the Members of the Seventy-seventh Congress, at a moment unprecedented in the history of the Union. I use the word "unprecedented," because at no previous time has American security been as seriously threatened from without as it is today. . . .

Therefore, as your President, performing my constitutional duty to "give to the Congress information of the state of the Union," I find it, unhappily, necessary to report that the future and the safety of our country and of our democracy are overwhelmingly involved in events far beyond our borders. . . .

We must all prepare to make the sacrifices that the emergency—almost as serious as war itself—demands. Whatever stands in the way of speed and efficiency in defense preparations must give way to the national need.

A free nation has the right to expect full cooperation from all groups. A free nation has the right to look to the leaders of business, of labor, and

Franklin Roosevelt was the only president to be elected four times. A Constitutional amendment ratified in 1951, six years after Roosevelt's death, now prevents individuals from being elected more than twice.

of agriculture to take the lead in stimulating effort, not among other groups but within their own groups. . . .

A part of the sacrifice means the payment of more money in taxes. In my Budget Message I shall recommend that a greater portion of this great defense program be paid for from taxation than we are paying today. No person should try, or be allowed, to get rich out of this program; and the principle of tax payments in accordance with ability to pay should be constantly before our eyes to guide our legislation.

If the Congress maintains these principles, the voters, putting patriotism ahead of pocketbooks, will give you their applause.

In the future days, which we seek to make secure, we look forward to a world founded upon four essential human freedoms.

The first is freedom of speech and expression—everywhere in the world.

The second is freedom of every person to worship God in his own way—everywhere in the world.

The third is freedom from want—which, translated into world terms, means economic understandings which will secure to every nation a healthy peacetime life for its inhabitants—everywhere in the world.

The fourth is freedom from fear—which, translated into world terms, means a world-wide reduction of armaments to such a point and in such a thorough fashion that no nation will be in a position to commit an act of physical aggression against any neighbor—anywhere in the world.

That is no vision of a distant millennium. It is a definite basis for a kind of world attainable in our own time and generation. That kind of world is the very antithesis[6] of the so-called new order of tyranny which the dictators seek to create with the crash of a bomb.

To that new order we oppose the greater conception—the moral order. A good society is able to face schemes of world domination and foreign revolutions alike without fear.

Since the beginning of our American history, we have been engaged in change—in a perpetual peaceful revolution—a revolution which goes on steadily, quietly adjusting itself to changing conditions—without the concentration camp or the quick-lime in the ditch. The world order which we seek is the cooperation of free countries, working together in a friendly, civilized society.

This nation has placed its destiny in the hands and heads and hearts of its millions of free men and women; and its faith in freedom under the guidance of God. Freedom means the supremacy of human rights everywhere. Our support goes to those who struggle to gain those rights or keep them. Our strength is our unity of purpose. To that high concept there can be no end save victory.

Ronald Reagan: The *Challenger* Speech

On the morning of January 28, 1986, millions of Americans were watching as the space shuttle Challenger *was launched. Then, 73 seconds after take-off, people watched in horror as the shuttle exploded and crashed into the ocean. All seven crew members died. That night, President Ronald Reagan addressed the nation. His speech is a classic example of how a president serves as the emotional leader of the country.*

Ladies and gentlemen, I'd planned to speak to you tonight to report on the state of the Union, but the events of earlier today have led me to change those plans. Today is a day for mourning and remembering. Nancy[7] and I are pained to the core by the tragedy of the shuttle *Challenger*. We know we share this pain with all of the people of our country. This is truly a national loss.

---

6 **antithesis:** opposite
7 **Nancy:** President Reagan's wife

Nineteen years ago, almost to the day, we lost three astronauts in a terrible accident on the ground. But we've never lost an astronaut in flight; we've never had a tragedy like this. And perhaps we've forgotten the courage it took for the crew of the shuttle. But they, the *Challenger* Seven, were aware of the dangers, but overcame them and did their jobs brilliantly. We mourn seven heroes: Michael Smith, Dick Scobee, Judith Resnik, Ronald McNair, Ellison Onizuka, Gregory Jarvis, and Christa McAuliffe. We mourn their loss as a nation together.

For the families of the seven, we cannot bear, as you do, the full impact of this tragedy. But we feel the loss, and we're thinking about you so very much. Your loved ones were daring and brave, and they had that special grace, that special spirit that says, "Give me a challenge, and I'll meet it with joy." They had a hunger to explore the universe and discover its truths. They wished to serve, and they did. They served all of us. We've grown used to wonders in this century. It's hard to dazzle us. But for 25 years the United States space program has been doing just that. We've grown used to the idea of space, and perhaps we forget that we've only just begun.

Ronald Reagan was known as "the Great Communicator" because he was such a skilled speaker.

We're still pioneers. They, the members of the *Challenger* crew, were pioneers.

And I want to say something to the schoolchildren of America who were watching the live coverage of the shuttle's takeoff. I know it is hard to understand, but sometimes painful things like this happen. It's all part of the process of exploration and discovery. It's all part of taking a chance and expanding man's horizons. The future doesn't belong to the fainthearted; it belongs to the brave. The *Challenger* crew was pulling us into the future, and we'll continue to follow them.

I've always had great faith in and respect for our space program, and what happened today does nothing to diminish it. We don't hide our space program. We don't keep secrets and cover things up. We do it all up front and in public. That's the way freedom is, and we wouldn't change it for a minute. We'll continue our quest in space. There will be more shuttle flights and more shuttle crews and, yes, more volunteers, more civilians, more teachers in space. Nothing ends here; our hopes and our journeys continue. I want to add that I wish I could talk to every man and woman who works for NASA or who worked on this mission and tell them: "Your dedication and professionalism have moved and impressed us for decades. And we know of your anguish.[8] We share it."

There's a coincidence today. On this day 390 years ago, the great explorer Sir Francis Drake died aboard ship off the coast of Panama. In his lifetime the great frontiers were the oceans, and a historian later said, "He lived by the sea, died on it, and was buried in it." Well, today we can say of the *Challenger* crew: Their dedication was, like Drake's, complete.

The crew of the space shuttle *Challenger* honored us by the manner in which they lived their lives. We will never forget them, nor the last time we saw them, this morning, as they prepared for their journey and waved goodbye and "slipped the surly[9] bonds of earth" to "touch the face of God."[10]

---

8 **anguish:** mental pain
9 **surly:** unfriendly or grouchy
10 **"slipped . . . God":** words from "High Flight," a poem by John Magee, Jr.

The Greatness of Lincoln

Vachel Lindsay

Historians, psychologists, novelists, and others have studied why some individuals succeed more than others do in the presidency. In the following poems, Vachel Lindsay describes two of the personality traits that he believes made Lincoln a great president.

Abraham Lincoln Walks at Midnight

It is portentous,[1] and a thing of state
That here at midnight, in our little town
A mourning figure walks, and will not rest,
Near the old court-house pacing up and down.

Or by his homestead, or in shadowed yards
He lingers where his children used to play,
Or through the market, on the well-worn stones
He stalks until the dawn-stars burn away.

A bronzed, lank man! His suit of ancient black,
A famous high top-hat and plain worn shawl
Make him the quaint great figure that men love,
The prairie-lawyer, master of us all.

He cannot sleep upon his hillside now.
He is among us:—as in times before!
And we who toss and lie awake for long
Breathe deep, and start, to see him pass the door.

---

1 **portentous:** significant, indicating something important

His head is bowed. He thinks on men and kings.
Yea, when the sick world cries, how can he sleep?
Too many peasants fight, they know not why,
Too many homesteads in black terror weep.

The sins of all the war-lords burn his heart.
He sees the dreadnaughts[2] scouring every main.[3]
He carries on his shawl-wrapped shoulders now
The bitterness, the folly and the pain.

He cannot rest until a spirit-dawn
Shall come;—the shining hope of Europe free;
The league of sober folk, the Workers' Earth,
Bringing long peace to Cornland, Alp and Sea.

It breaks his heart that kings must murder still,
That all his hours of travail[4] here for men
Seem yet in vain. And who will bring white peace
That he may sleep upon his hill again?

Lincoln

Would I might rouse[5] the Lincoln in you all,
That which is gendered[6] in the wilderness
From lonely prairies and God's tenderness.
Imperial soul, star of a weedy stream,
Born where the ghosts of buffaloes still dream,
Whose spirit hoof-beats storm above his grave,
Above that breast of earth and prairie-fire—
Fire that freed the slave.

---

2 **dreadnaughts:** war ships
3 **main:** sea
4 **travail:** hard work or suffering
5 **rouse:** stir up or awaken
6 **gendered:** produced

The President as Teacher-in-Chief

Rudy Ruiz

More than a century ago, President Theodore Roosevelt described the presidency as a "bully pulpit." He believed that an energetic president had a platform on which to speak to, and inspire, everyone in the nation. Journalist Rudy Ruiz looks at whether a president can still use the bully pulpit today.

Perhaps we got too used to living in a nation where the president inevitably becomes persona non grata.[1]

Maybe after the Clinton and Bush years, we forgot how to give a president a chance to serve not just as a punching bag but also as a role model.

Have we become so disenchanted and polarized [that] we can't give our own president a chance to teach our children something about what it takes to succeed?

As a small-town boy, I drew inspiration from presidential biographies. As I got lost in the adventures of Teddy Roosevelt, the spirit of George Washington, and the ideals of Thomas Jefferson, I found kernels of America's greatness. In those pages, I unearthed a yearning to dream beyond my surroundings, to strive for more, to seek a way to contribute to our nation.

Many of the leaders, including Abraham Lincoln, born in a log cabin in Kentucky, ascended from humble beginnings on the wings of education to guide America forward. Devouring their stories, it ceased to matter where I was from or how far removed I was from the centers of power. With an education and a dream—in America—anything was possible.

---

1 **persona non grata:** an unwelcomed or disrespected person

Theodore Roosevelt, who served as president from 1901 to 1909, was famous for his impassioned speaking style.

Whenever President Obama addresses our youth, he embodies the power of education. Education is the cornerstone of our democracy, the key to upward mobility, a linchpin to transforming whimsical dreams into actionable goals.

Ask Bill Clinton. Raised by his widowed mother in Arkansas, he became a Rhodes Scholar. Look at Barack Obama. Emerging from a broken family, he built on degrees from Columbia and Harvard in his odyssey to the White House.

Remember Dwight Eisenhower. Hailing from Kansas, he attended West Point on his way to heroism. From both sides of the aisle, education has propelled the career trajectories of our nation's leaders.

Even if we disagree with a president's policies, we should accept he can serve as a role model in a broader way. For example, Thomas Jefferson owned slaves. Nobody would argue this was admirable. But Jefferson was also a great thinker, diplomat, and strategist.

He co-authored the Declaration of Independence and helped America become a global power by engaging Europe and transacting the Louisiana Purchase. Was he perfect? Of course not. Would we want our children to emulate[2] his every action? No way. But has he been an inspirational role model over time.

As a parent, I understand people's concerns about the concepts to which their children are exposed. But the content of the president's speech[3] to students should assuage[4] any worries regarding his motives.

Clearly, his agenda is to inspire kids to make the most of education in building a better life, not to brainwash a generation to do his bidding. Pointing to his own experiences, as well as those of others from diverse and modest origins, his remarks convey the importance of personal responsibility, perseverance, and education in fulfilling one's potential while contributing to our nation's future.

The only way to argue with that is by confusing the issues, twisting the situation into something it was never intended to be. It's gotten so bad, some folks don't want their kids exposed to the president because they're afraid he'll teach them socialism. My answer is that even if he did plan to discuss socialism, they should let their child listen. Of course, the president wouldn't do that, but why is that my answer?

---

2 **emulate:** act the same way

3 **president's speech:** On September 8, 2009, President Obama spoke to students upon their return to school. Before the speech, some people criticized it, charging that it would be political.

4 **assuage:** ease or moderate

Because, as another role model—President Reagan—once said: "All great change in America begins at the dinner table."

In that light, the president's speech isn't a threat but an opportunity for families to engage their children on the issues. If parents disagree with the president's views, they can sit down at the dinner table with their kids and explain their divergence.[5] They may even find, when it comes to the value of education, President Obama might say something worth hearing. In the process, parents will teach their children:

- That we should listen respectfully to others. Doing so, we might realize that we can appreciate certain aspects of a person while disagreeing with others, and that partial differences of opinion needn't always spur absolute rejection.

- That we should respect the president because, even if we didn't vote for him, we're still one nation.

- That we should give our president an opportunity to lead by example.

Obama's presidency is still young. We don't know what shape his legacy will take. But given his resume, regardless of politics, he's an excellent role model on the value of education. Why not give him a chance to serve in that capacity?

Just as I found inspiration in those biographies during my childhood, our youth might be moved by the president's words and stories to cherish knowledge and learning, harnessing the power of education to grow into productive, exemplary Americans in their own right.

---

5 **divergence:** difference of direction or opinion

Listen Up, Mr. President

Helen Thomas and Craig Crawford

Part of the success of a president is an ability to connect with a broad range of citizens. Voters expect presidents to know something about almost everything. They need to identify policies that promote economic growth, keep peace with other countries, and protect individual liberties. In addition, people expect them to comment on college basketball, host classical violinists at the White House, and know the price of a gallon of milk. To help incoming presidents achieve success, veteran news reporter Helen Thomas and co-author Craig Crawford provide some advice for presidents.

Above Us, Yet Among Us

Great presidents tend to be those who inspire by being who Americans aspire to be, while also seeming to be one of the people. The presidency is an exalted position, to be sure, but getting too used to the high altitude of that lofty pedestal can ensure that one day you will be knocked down from it.

One of our most popular and successful presidents, Franklin D. Roosevelt, was raised in wealthy privilege far beyond anything average Americans could imagine, then or now. And yet most citizens believed he truly understood their concerns thanks to an uncanny knack for speaking their language. Historians speculate that Roosevelt partly learned this skill in Warm Springs, Georgia, where, to the horror of his rich family, he chose to recuperate from his crippling polio, trying to learn to walk again surrounded by lower-class and rural people.

In a letter to his wife, Eleanor, from Warm Springs, FDR wrote of his awakening to the plight of poor people that "rattles my soul." In a fitting completion of the unique circle of his life, Roosevelt died there at the end of one of the greatest presidencies in American history.

Presidential Approval Ratings				
President	Term	Lowest	Highest	Average
Harry Truman	1945–1953	22	87	45
Dwight Eisenhower	1953–1961	48	79	65
John Kennedy	1961–1963	56	83	70
Lyndon Johnson	1963–1969	35	79	55
Richard Nixon	1969–1974	24	67	49
Gerald Ford	1974–1977	37	71	47
Jimmy Carter	1977–1981	28	75	46
Ronald Reagan	1981–1989	35	68	53
George H. W. Bush	1989–1993	29	89	61
Bill Clinton	1993–2001	37	73	55
George W. Bush	2001–2009	25	90	49
Barack Obama	2009–2011	38	69	49

Source: Gallup, Inc.

The ratings in this table indicate the percentage of people who gave the president a favorable rating at different points during his time in office. What generalizations can you make about the public attitude toward presidents?

Ronald Reagan was another widely popular president with a common touch despite a glamorous life as a Hollywood actor. In his case, Reagan's simpatico[1] with average Americans stemmed from a typically middle-class upbringing in Illinois.

Voters should not overdo demanding the common touch if it comes with a lack of other important skills. It is often said during campaigns that a winning candidate is the one with whom most voters would "want to have a beer." The down-to-earth person who seems most like the rest of us. Putting aside the fact that few Americans will ever get such a chance, going too far with such an average standard would mean that we'd end up with a lot of mediocre presidents.

After all, it is unlikely that the average American would make a good president.

Being above us, and yet one of us, is perhaps your toughest challenge, Mr. President, and failing to meet it is a big reason so many of your predecessors left office in shame or regret.

"You Are the One in Trouble Now"

Remaining keenly aware of the struggles and troubles ahead, without being consumed by them, should keep you grounded in reality, Mr. President. It might even help you avoid getting blindsided by a crisis that you could have seen coming.

---

1 **simpatico:** similar feeling or outlook

Many presidents learn the hard way just how demanding and difficult the job can be. It can be so awful that you have to wonder why dozens of seemingly sane people run for the job every four years. More than a few who actually won the office at times pondered whether it was worth it.

At the outset of what would be a grueling twenty-two-month campaign to become the nation's forty-fourth president, Barack Obama seemed unsure to aides. Some wondered if he really wanted it bad enough when the Illinois senator asked what sounded like a naive[2] question.

"Will I be able to take weekends off?" the Democrat pondered aloud. Obama soon learned that presidential candidates—and especially presidents—get precious few weekend furloughs.[3]

Vice presidents who unexpectedly ascended to the presidency without the long campaigns that prepare one for the rigors of office soon became acutely aware of what they inherited.

On April 12, 1945, the day President Roosevelt passed away, his vice president, Harry S. Truman, remarked to reporters, "Pray for me, boys, the moon and the stars just fell on me."

Those in Truman's situation often provoked pity from those who really knew what they were in for. Also on that fateful day in 1945, FDR's grieving widow demonstrated that she felt even sorrier for what awaited the man who would succeed him.

Truman was a bit stunned by the reaction he got from First Lady Eleanor Roosevelt as he offered consolation. "Is there anything I can do for you?" Truman asked.

Without a pause, Mrs. Roosevelt brushed aside Truman's concern, saying, "Is there anything we can do for you? For you are the one in trouble now."

It wasn't so much that Mrs. Roosevelt felt the times were especially tough for the new president. World War II was winding down and the nation's economy was on the upswing. She was really referring to the pressures of a job that is overwhelming in the best of times.

Just a week or so after that initial exchange, Mrs. Roosevelt sent a handwritten letter to Truman expanding upon her warning. Enclosing one her husband's favorite figurines, a comical-looking donkey, Mrs. Roosevelt wrote, "This little donkey has long been in my husband's

---

2 **naive:** lacking understanding about the world
3 **furloughs:** vacations or temporary breaks from responsibility

Eleanor Roosevelt and Harry Truman, shown here at Franklin Roosevelt's gravesite, provided support for each other.

possession and was on his desk. He looks a bit obstinate[4] and Franklin said he needed a reminder sometimes that his decisions had to be final and taken with a sense that God would give guidance to a humble beast. Once having decided something, the obstinate little donkey kept his sense of humor and determination going against great pressure."

Truman wrote back about the donkey, "He certainly is in a typical mulish attitude and, as the President used to say, when I have a hard decision to make I will look at him, think of you and the President, and then try to make the best decision."

Mrs. Roosevelt's early thoughts about Truman's needs apply to all new presidents.

---

4 **obstinate:** stubborn

You are still a "humble beast," Mr. President, just a human being who will make mistakes. You will face great pressure and will very much need to keep a sense of humor. . . .

Choose Your Model

Presidential scholar James MacGregor Burns has written extensively about three basic categories for presidential governing. Presidents generally fall under one of three models (even though they might occasionally deploy the others in certain circumstances):

- Madisonian Model: A principal architect of the Constitution, James Madison was faithful to the document's intent that the president rely on Congress to lead in setting policy. The president mainly administers policies set by Congress.

- Hamiltonian Model: Alexander Hamilton, also a constitutional author, held a very different view from Madison's. The president should be heroic and above partisanship, relying on public opinion for support and ignoring Congress if necessary.

- Jeffersonian Model: Thomas Jefferson's approach to the presidency relied on the support of his political party. His model would have the president act in similar ways to a prime minister in a parliamentary system.[5] The party, influenced and led by the president, sets policy. The president assists the party with getting its members' platform enacted.

Madisonian presidents tend to be incremental[6] managers who do not leave much of a legacy for the history books, which is probably why modern occupants of the White House steer clear of the Congress-first example, even if that is more faithful to what the Constitution intended.

Historians consider William Howard Taft[7] probably our last Madisonian president. More of a legal technician than a skilled political actor, Taft approached governing like a Swiss watch, working the levers of our system of checks and balances with precision. Still, he was not one to sit

---

5 **parliamentary system:** a form of government, common in Europe, in which the dominant party in the legislature chooses one of the legislators to serve as chief executive
6 **incremental:** characterized by small, gradual change
7 **William Howard Taft:** president of the United States, 1909 to 1913

and wait for congressional authority to *execute* his powers. Taft got quite a bit done, such as instituting the income tax, expanding civil service, strengthening the Interstate Commerce Commission, and significantly improving the postal system.

Jeffersonian presidents like Woodrow Wilson[8] got much done by expertly using their role as party leaders to steer Congress, but in the end these powers failed him in his vain[9] efforts to create a League of Nations[10]—so much so that he suffered a debilitating stroke while barnstorming the country to campaign for it.

Wilson was such an admirer of Jeffersonian-style party rule that early in his political career he advocated a change to the Constitution to create a parliamentary-style government, replacing popularly elected presidents with a prime minister chosen by the majority party in Congress. By the time he was president, however, Wilson had changed his mind. Eventually, he came around to the prevailing view, more or less defining the modern presidency by saying that it "will be as big as and as influential as the man who occupies it."

Heroic presidents of the Hamiltonian type are now the norm, although the overreaching and power-grabbing that often comes with this style causes some to end up as villains to many Americans. We now look to them for leadership and results beyond anything the job was actually created to achieve.

The two Roosevelts, Theodore and Franklin, and John F. Kennedy set the Hamiltonian model in stone. Their inspirational eloquence and charismatic personalities produced a power base of popular appeal that at times made Congress seem almost irrelevant to most citizens—even if it wasn't.

---

8   **Woodrow Wilson:** president of the United States, 1913 to 1921
9   **vain:** unsuccessful
10 **League of Nations:** an organization of countries proposed by Wilson that he hoped would keep world peace, but that Congress did not ratify joining

Responding to Cluster Two

What Makes a President Great?
Critical Thinking Skill EVALUATING ARGUMENTS

1. Analyze the claim made by Akhil Reed Amar that presidents are expected to think and act independently. Use the chart below to identify and evaluate the effectiveness of the reasons, examples, and quotations included in the writer's argument.

Reason/Example/Quotation	Evaluation

2. Evaluate Washington's claim that the United States' "detached and distant situation invites and enables us to pursue a different course." Contrast his attitude toward foreign policy with that expressed by Franklin Roosevelt.

3. Identify the concepts and language that make Abraham Lincoln's "Gettysburg Address" so powerful. Analyze Lincoln's personality as presented in the Lindsay poems.

4. Compare the idea of freedom expressed by Franklin Roosevelt and Ronald Reagan. Evaluate which one you find more persuasive.

5. Evaluate Rudy Ruiz's argument about the power of education in a democracy. Explain whether he is persuasive.

6. What reasons does Helen Thomas use to support her argument that a president's greatest challenge is "being above us, and yet one of us"?

Writing Activity: Present an Argument in a Speech

Write a three-minute speech arguing for three qualities that make a president great. Include examples describing at least three presidents. Present your speech to the class. Your classmates should evaluate both the content and presentation of your speech.

A Strong Expository Speech

- clearly presents the main points

- includes well-chosen supporting examples and details

- is presented using appropriate eye contact, volume, and pronunciation

CLUSTER THREE

How Does the Supreme Court Effect Change?

Critical Thinking Skill SUMMARIZING KEY IDEAS

THE LEAST DANGEROUS BRANCH

ALEXANDER HAMILTON

The United States Constitution was written in 1787. Before it took effect, though, the states had to ratify it. In several states, including New York, the battle over ratification was close and hard-fought. To win support for the proposed Constitution, James Madison, Alexander Hamilton, and John Jay wrote a series of more than 80 essays and published them in newspapers. These essays, now called The Federalist, *provide insight into what some of the Founders believed the Constitution meant. In essay number 78, Hamilton examines the power of the judiciary.*

To the People of the State of New York:

WE PROCEED now to an examination of the judiciary department of the proposed government. . . .

According to the plan of the convention, all judges who may be appointed by the United States are to hold their offices DURING GOOD BEHAVIOR; which is conformable to the most approved of the State constitutions and among the rest, to that of this State [New York]. . . .

Whoever attentively considers the different departments of power must perceive that, in a government in which they are separated from each other, the judiciary, from the nature of its functions, will always be the least dangerous to the political rights of the Constitution; because it will be least in a capacity to annoy or injure them. The Executive not only dispenses the honors, but holds the sword of the community. The legislature not only commands the purse, but prescribes the rules by which the duties and rights of every citizen are to be regulated. The judiciary, on the contrary, has no influence over either the sword or the purse; no direction either of the strength or of the wealth of the society; and can take no active resolution whatever. It may truly be said to have neither FORCE nor WILL, but merely judgment; and must ultimately depend upon the aid of the executive arm even for the efficacy of its judgments. . . .

The complete independence of the courts of justice is peculiarly essential in a limited Constitution. By a limited Constitution, I understand one which contains certain specified exceptions to the legislative authority; such, for instance, as that it shall pass no bills of attainder,[1] no ex-post-facto laws,[2] and the like. Limitations of this kind can be preserved in practice no other way than through the medium of courts of justice, whose duty it must be to declare all acts contrary to the manifest tenor of the Constitution void. Without this, all the reservations of particular rights or privileges would amount to nothing. . . .

[T]he courts were designed to be an intermediate body between the people and the legislature, in order, among other things, to keep the latter within the limits assigned to their authority. The interpretation of the laws is the proper and peculiar province of the courts. A constitution is, in fact, and must be regarded by the judges, as a fundamental law. It therefore belongs to them to ascertain[3] its meaning, as well as the meaning of any particular act proceeding from the legislative body. If there should happen to be an irreconcilable variance between the two, that which has the superior obligation and validity ought, of course, to be preferred; or, in other words, the Constitution ought to be preferred to the statute, the intention of the people to the intention of their agents.

"Mr. Justice, must you keep repeating 'nobody can fire me, nobody can fire me, nobody can fire me'?"

What are the costs and the benefits of lifetime appointments for justices?

---

1 **bill of attainder:** a law that convicts an individual of a crime
2 **ex-post-facto law:** a law that punishes people for acts done before the law was passed
3 **ascertain:** evaluate and decide

DEFENDERS AGAINST TYRANNY

ALEXIS DE TOCQUEVILLE

Alexis de Tocqueville was supposed to be studying the prison system in the United States when he came from France for a tour in 1831. Actually, he had another purpose. Tocqueville came from a wealthy family of nobles, but he could see that democracy and equality were spreading rapidly in Europe and the Americas. He wanted to understand these new ideas. He was curious about how they affected manners, morals, and government in the United States. The book he wrote about his observations, Democracy in America, *became the most influential commentary about American culture ever written by a foreigner.*

In the United States the Constitution governs the legislator as much as the private citizen: as it is the first of laws, it cannot be modified by a law; and it is therefore just that the tribunals[1] should obey the Constitution in preference to any law. This condition belongs to the very essence of the judicature;[2] for to select that legal obligation by which he is most strictly bound is in some sort the natural right of every magistrate.

In France the constitution is also the first of laws, and the judges have the same right to take it as the ground of their decisions; but were they to exercise this right, they must perforce[3] encroach[4] on rights more sacred than their own: namely, on those of society, in whose name they are acting. In this case reasons of state clearly prevail over ordinary motives. In America, where the nation can always reduce its magistrates to obedience by changing its Constitution, no danger of this kind is to be feared. Upon this point, therefore, the political and the logical reason agree, and the people as well as the judges preserve their privileges.

---

1 **tribunals:** judges and justices
2 **judicature:** system of courts and judges
3 **perforce:** necessarily
4 **encroach:** invade

Whenever a law that the judge holds to be unconstitutional is invoked in a tribunal of the United States, he may refuse to admit it as a rule; this power is the only one peculiar to the American magistrate, but it gives rise to immense political influence. In truth, few laws can escape the searching analysis of the judicial power for any length of time,

"Social engineering" occurs when the government uses laws, policies, or court rulings to change how people behave. The phrase is generally used as a criticism.

for there are few that are not prejudicial[5] to some private interest or other, and none that may not be brought before a court of justice by the choice of parties or by the necessity of the case. But as soon as a judge has refused to apply any given law in a case, that law immediately loses a portion of its moral force. Those to whom it is prejudicial learn that means exist of overcoming its authority, and similar suits are multiplied until it becomes powerless. The alternative, then, is that the people must alter the Constitution or the legislature must repeal the law. The political power which the Americans have entrusted to their courts of justice is therefore immense, but the evils of this power are considerably diminished by the impossibility of attacking the laws except through the courts of justice. If the judge had been empowered to contest the law on the ground of theoretical generalities, if he were able to take the initiative and to censure[6] the legislator, he would play a prominent political part; and as the champion or the antagonist of a party, he would have brought the hostile passions of the nation into the conflict. But when a judge contests a law in an obscure debate on some particular case, the importance of his attack is concealed from public notice; his decision bears upon the interest of an individual, and the law is slighted only incidentally. Moreover, although it is censured, it is not abolished; its

---

5 **prejudicial:** in violation of
6 **censure:** criticize or limit the power of

moral force may be diminished but its authority is not taken away; and its final destruction can be accomplished only by the reiterated attacks of judicial functionaries. It will be seen, also, that by leaving it to private interest to censure the law, and by intimately uniting the trial of the law with the trial of an individual, legislation is protected from wanton[7] assaults and from the daily aggressions of party spirit. The errors of the legislator are exposed only to meet a real want; and it is always a positive and appreciable fact that must serve as the basis of a prosecution.

I am inclined to believe this practice of the American courts to be at once most favorable to liberty and to public order. If the judge could attack the legislator only openly and directly, he would sometimes be afraid to oppose him; and at other times party spirit might encourage him to brave it at every turn. The laws would consequently be attacked when the power from which they emanated was weak, and obeyed when it was strong; that is to say, when it would be useful to respect them, they would often be contested; and when it would be easy to convert them into an instrument of oppression, they would be respected. But the American judge is brought into the political arena independently of his own will. He judges the law only because he is obliged to judge a case. The political question that he is called upon to resolve is connected with the interests of the parties, and he cannot refuse to decide it without a denial of justice. He performs his functions as a citizen by fulfilling the precise duties which belong to his profession as a magistrate. It is true that, upon this system, the judicial censorship of the courts of justice over the legislature cannot extend to all laws indiscriminately, inasmuch as some of them can never give rise to that precise species of contest which is termed a lawsuit; and even when such a contest is possible, it may happen that no one cares to bring it before a court of justice. The Americans have often felt this inconvenience; but they have left the remedy incomplete, lest they should give it an efficacy that might in some cases prove dangerous. Within these limits the power vested in the American courts of justice of pronouncing a statute to be unconstitutional forms one of the most powerful barriers that have ever been devised against the tyranny of political assemblies.

---

7 **wanton:** irresponsible

The Weakness of Courts

Stephen L. Carter

In The Federalist, *Alexander Hamilton called the courts "the least dangerous branch" of government. Other leaders of his time, such as George Mason, disagreed. He viewed the courts as a threat to individual liberties. People have debated ever since whether the judicial branch of government is more likely to protect liberties or to destroy them. Stephen L. Carter considers how the Supreme Court exerts its power under the U.S. Constitution.*

Yet popular rhetoric about the courts suggests that they are places to which citizens can repair[1] for redress[2] when the "government"—again, somehow defined as excluding judges—has denied them their rights.

Nevertheless, it should be plain that courts cannot really play this role. Remember what I pointed out earlier, and what Dr. King never forgot—that the courts are simply an arm of the state. But they are not like the other arms, and the judges know it. And the ways in which they are different help explain why, in cases of genuine dissensus,[3] the judiciary cannot operate as a significant check on the other branches.

How is being a judge different? But for our post-civil-rights love affair with judicial power, the answer would be obvious. A judge can tell people what to do, but the people might not do what they are told. And if the people refuse to do what they are told, there is little that the judge can do about it—not, at least, without the aid of another, more powerful branch of government. The legal scholar Arthur Leff once wrote that behind every judicial decision stands the massed might of the 82nd Airborne.[4] But Leff was writing tongue-in-cheek, for he plainly recognized that the claim is not quite true. The 82nd Airborne stands behind the

---

1   **repair:** go to
2   **redress:** relief or remedy
3   **dissensus:** disagreement among people
4   **82nd Airborne:** a famous division of the United States Army

judicial opinion only if the troops are ordered to go—and a judge cannot give that order.

The simple truth is that judges have few weapons other than their own prestige with which to force compliance with their edicts. Alexander Bickel[5] pressed this point quite eloquently a generation ago, but today's constitutional theorists seem to find it a little bit embarrassing. Nowadays, legal scholars rarely try to link theories of adjudication[6] to theories of political obligation. The shelves of the nation's law libraries are lined with sophisticated arguments on why judges should adopt one interpretive approach or another when confronting constitutional questions, but very few of the authors bother to explain why, if the judge follows the method advocated, anybody should pay attention. Smart scholars have argued for constitutional rights to everything from health care to drug use to nonpayment of taxes, and some of the arguments are quite engaging; but constitutional theory, as a body, gives inadequate attention to what it is that turns a judicial "opinion," as a court's written product is so honestly called, into a lawgiving event.

Not only is constitutional theory embarrassed by this omission—so are the judges themselves. True, judicial opinions almost never make explicit references to the possibility of disobedience; and, when they do, it is almost always in condemnation, as one would expect. The thundering anathema[7] at the very idea of defiance has worked its way into our political language, I suspect, largely because of its relentless repetition by the courts which, during the civil rights era, millions of Americans sensibly came to love. But the fact that judges

What do you think this image implies about the power of the judiciary?

---

5 **Alexander Bickel:** an influential Constitutional scholar who lived from 1924 to 1974

6 **adjudication:** the process a judge uses to make a decision

7 **anathema:** criticism for being immoral or improper

express no doubts that their decisions (that is, opinions) will be obeyed should not be taken to mean that they harbor none. And there are, from time to time, moments of quite astonishing judicial honesty. One is the Supreme Court's 1876 decision in *Mississippi v. Johnson,* in which the Justices declined to issue an order prohibiting President Andrew Johnson from enforcing the Reconstruction Acts. The stated ground was enchantingly straightforward: "If the President refuse obedience, it is needless to observe that the court is without power to enforce its process."

But such frank discussions of judicial weakness are rare events, even though we have known, at least since the pioneering work of Bickel in the sixties, of the many indirect ways in which judges incorporate into their opinions their self-knowledge of weakness. Bickel pointed out that the courts often use such amorphous [vague] doctrines as standing, justiciability, mootness, and ripeness[8] to avoid deciding those things they would rather not decide—and that the prudence of deciding not to decide is often a matter of preserving scarce judicial capital for the next (perhaps more important) battle.

Contemporary scholars look askance [with scorn] at Bickel, who is seen as misunderstanding the judicial responsibility to decide questions properly put. To the bloodless technocrat, this may seem to be precisely right. To the ruthless promoter of causes, Bickel may even seem a bit reactionary, not to say cowardly. But today's theorists often forget that Bickel pointed to the inherent weakness of the judiciary in order to *defend* the courts against mainstream critics who considered the desegregation decision[9] an illegitimate power-grab: the courts, he meant his readers to understand, were not "dangerous." Bickel's genius came in his recognizing what modern theory would rather ignore: it is not obvious that people will obey judicial opinions that are wrong-headed, and even less obvious that they should. The "passive virtues," as Bickel called them, enable the courts to avoid squandering their legitimacy by seeming to find constitutional rights everywhere. Or they did perform that function, in the days when judicial hubris [excessive pride] was less than it is now.

---

8 **standing, justiciability, mootness, and ripeness:** four principles used by judges to help them decide whether they should rule a case

9 **desegregation decision:** the Supreme Court's 1954 decision in *Brown v. Board of Education* that ruled that states could not mandate segregation in schools

Friends and Foes on the Supreme Court

Kevin Merida and Michael A. Fletcher

No work environment is quite like that of the United States Supreme Court. While each of the nine justices works with a separate team of clerks, all nine must come together to decide a case. Their decisions are often based on narrow, technical points of law. However, they also reflect fundamental views of government, public life, and ethics. It is through these decisions that the justices exert their power.

The Supreme Court can be a lonely place for a justice. Clarence Thomas had no idea. Getting there [in 1991] was such a huge triumph that the isolation took him by surprise. The work of judges—consulting law books, reading case files, writing opinions—is by its nature solitary. But Thomas had not anticipated such little interaction with his brethren. Justices rarely visit one another, and hardly ever unannounced. Mainly they see one another during their twice weekly conferences to review cases or when they are on the bench listening to oral arguments, which occur during two weeks of each month from October through April, and then only on Mondays, Tuesdays, and Wednesdays.

The justices also don't have much phone contact, communicating primarily by memo and through their law clerks. The oft-used metaphor that the court is like nine independent law firms especially resonates with Thomas, and not in a good way. Thomas has joked that the communication he receives from colleagues is "usually a letter such as, 'Dear Clarence, I disagree with everything in your opinion except your name . . . Cheers.'" Jokes aside, Thomas is a social creature, and the court's stiff culture is frustrating at times.

A visitor who joined Thomas for lunch in his chambers not long ago was struck by how lukewarm Thomas seemed about his work life. The visitor had asked a simple question: "How was the job going?" To which Thomas replied, "Okay." Okay? Some lawyers spend their entire lives dreaming of being nominated to the Supreme Court. The visitor decided to pursue whether Thomas was actually happy as a justice. Would he rather be doing something else? Yes, Thomas said, he'd rather be a small businessman like his grandfather Myers Anderson. He'd rather own something or work with his hands, Thomas told this visitor.

Occasionally Thomas has thought he just doesn't fit in with the other justices. He is not particularly comfortable at official court functions. He is not an opera fan like Ginsburg and Scalia. He doesn't play poker or bridge, and everyone seemed to play bridge: Breyer, Rehnquist, Kennedy, O'Connor. All participated in a rotating, high-powered Washington bridge game. Thomas considered these the hobbies of the ruling class. One of the reasons Thomas never took up golf—Kennedy and Stevens played, as did some of his friends—is because he views golf as a rich man's sport. He likes to curl up in front of his sixty-five-inch color TV and watch football. Until he tore his Achilles tendon in a 1993 pickup game, Thomas regularly played basketball with the clerks in the gym known as the "highest court in the land." He has played less frequently since his injury. "That's how I spent my last hour [as a law clerk], playing him one on one," said the six-foot-seven Stephen F. Smith, who clerked for Thomas during the 1993–94 term. "He was quite good."

Though he has boasted he will serve on the court for fifty years, just to outlive his critics, Thomas sometimes sounds like a restless soul. "I'm a lousy career planner,'" he once said. "I tried to map things out. I was going to be a millionaire by the time I was thirty."

In some ways, the high court is the strangest institution in our national government. "To the public at large, the Supreme Court is a remote and mysterious oracle that makes occasional pronouncements on major issues of the day and then disappears from view for months at a time," wrote Linda Greenhouse, the longtime *New York Times* Supreme Court reporter, in a *Yale Law Journal* article. "The nine individuals who exercise power in its name are unaccountable and essentially faceless." They don't hold news conferences to explain their opinions. They rarely respond to criticism—or even to errors made in reporting their rulings. You are not likely to bump into a justice at the Supreme Court, as you might a congressman at the U.S. Capitol. Even though there are only nine of them, justices often go unrecognized at restaurants and social events. A 2004 *Washington Post* poll showed that even Thomas, perhaps the court's most recognizable figure, remained largely unknown to about half of those surveyed.

Members of the Supreme Court are not well known as individuals. Polls generally show that less than half of the population can name any one of the nine justices.

Justices, for the most part, are not yearning for attention. They give speeches but don't release their public schedules. Thus, it is difficult to track their appearances. Most don't even bother sharing texts of their speeches with the Supreme Court's public information office for posting on the court's official Web site. So sensitive are they about how their words will be interpreted that some justices have actually discouraged universities or organizations from producing transcripts of their remarks.

"In a perfect world, I would never give another speech, address, talk, lecture or whatever as long as I live," wrote Justice Souter in a 1996 letter to his colleague Harry Blackmun. Needling Blackmun, he added: "I know you get a kick out of these things, but you have to realize that God gave you an element of sociability, and I think he gave you the share otherwise reserved for me." True, Souter is the court's most reclusive[1] member. He brings his lunch to work, typically yogurt and an apple, and enjoys the lonely hobby of running—he was once mugged while jogging in his Capitol Hill neighborhood. But even the outgoing Thomas, who gives remarkably self-revealing talks, has questioned whether he should continue making speeches. "Every time we open our mouths, we come close to compromising what we do," he told the Richmond Bar Association.

Under Chief Justice John Roberts, there are indications that the court is slowly moving away from some of its outdated practices. Transcripts of oral arguments, which used to take ten days to produce, are now available online within hours. That said, even with technological improvements—improvements Thomas has championed—the court is still something of an anachronism.[2] Karl Brooks, an associate professor of history and environmental studies at the University of Kansas, was reminded of this several years ago when he was a Supreme Court fellow. The fellows[3] program selects academics, attorneys, congressional aides, and others interested in taking a year off to plow into the work of the federal judiciary. One of the first things Brooks noticed was that the high court dealt almost exclusively in paper, when virtually all federal courts were allowing extensive filings by e-mail. . . .

The court is wedded to tradition. The justices don their black robes in what is known as the "robing room," a version of which has existed since 1860, when the court was located in what is now the Old Senate Chamber in the U.S. Capitol. The robes are hung in wooden lockers like uniforms. Such traditions foster collegiality, some justices believe. Chief Justice Warren Burger introduced the custom of celebrating justices' birthdays with a group lunch, a toast, and the singing of "Happy Birthday." According to John Paul Stevens, the court's most tenured justice, Thomas has "significantly improved the quality of our singing."

Thomas wants badly to belong, and no other justice speaks more glowingly of the court's traditions, especially its tradition of decorum. "Unlike so much of what we see in a contentious society, at least there, right or wrong, agree or disagree, there is the appropriate solemnity and gravitas[4] to what we do," he told students at Ohio's Ashland University

---

1 **reclusive:** seeking isolation from other people
2 **anachronism:** something that is out of place historically
3 **fellows:** distinguished individuals
4 **gravitas:** seriousness

in 1999. "And in a cynical environment, we see no cynicism. Never. Not one drop." Asked about his relationships with other justices, he said: "It is very warm, very respectful. There are no cliques,[5] there are no cabals,[6] there are no little work groups that sneak off and conspire against other people."

This is the Thomas who knows all too well the kind of brass-knuckle infighting that takes place in the executive and legislative branches of government. In fact, he is still somewhat engaged in the skirmishing, regularly representing the Supreme Court in congressional appropriations hearings about the court's budget. But the court is hardly, as Thomas depicts it, a bastion of genteel[7] deliberation, where an unkind word is seldom spoken and lobbying to win the support of justices is frowned upon.

That image was punctured by the 2004 release of the late justice Harry Blackmun's papers, which offer a rare glimpse into the relationship between a junior justice and his senior colleague. Blackmun's files

' 'Congress shall make no law'. . . now, I wonder what they meant by that . . .?'

"Congress shall make no law" is the beginning of the First Amendment. This is the amendment that protects the freedom of speech and other civil liberties. What do you think the cartoonist is saying about interpreting the Constitution?

---

5   **clique:** a small group of people who share an interest
6   **cabal:** a group of people, often secretly trying to gain power
7   **genteel:** polite and elegant

highlight the irreverence, pique,[8] and backstage political maneuvering that the court likes to pretend doesn't exist. Blackmun, who retired in 1994 after twenty-four years on the court, served with Thomas for three of those years. Though they were often on opposing sides of decisions, Thomas had an affinity for Blackmun because of their shared working-class roots. In July 2001, Thomas spoke at the dedication of the Harry A. Blackmun Rotunda in the federal courthouse in St. Louis. He noted that Blackmun was "a modest but unpretentious man" who drove a blue Volkswagen Beetle and would introduce himself to suburban fast-food patrons as "Harry, I work for the government."

A review of Blackmun's papers suggests, however, that he didn't think much of Thomas. He cataloged the bad press Thomas received, made snide remarks about some of Thomas's draft opinions "pretty bad," he noted of one and was annoyed by Thomas's most influential mentor, the prickly economist Thomas Sowell. In perhaps the most

Justices Stephen Breyer (left) and Antonin Scalia (right) get along very well, but they interpret the Constitution very differently. During the 2010–11 session, in decisions on which the Supreme Court was divided, Breyer and Scalia disagreed 67 percent of the time.

---

8 **pique:** resentment or frustration

intriguing correspondence between the two justices, Blackmun sent Thomas a copy of a biting column Sowell had written about Blackmun's announced opposition to the death penalty. "If this were just a case of one vain and shallow old man whom the media have puffed up for their own ideological reasons, it would hardly be worth noticing," Sowell wrote. "But Blackmun is a tawdry[9] symbol of what has gone so wrong in American law over the past few decades." Blackmun must have known how close Thomas was to Sowell when he forwarded the column to his fellow justice. Thomas has publicly referred to Sowell, a senior fellow at Stanford University's Hoover Institution, as "a dear friend" and someone who has had a profound impact on his thinking. Blackmun, nevertheless, in his March 18, 1994, letter to Thomas, said he had never heard of Sowell and proceeded to dress him down. "It is hard for me to understand," Blackmun wrote, "why a responsible university would employ one who dispenses material of this kind." Thomas was embarrassed. Three days later, he responded to Blackmun with a hand-written note, saying he had attempted to contact Sowell but had not yet reached him. "It is upsetting to me to see any friend of mine cause you such distress!" Thomas wrote. "I will speak with him." It's unclear whether Thomas ever spoke to Sowell about the column. (Sowell did not respond to repeated requests from us for an interview.) What is clear, though, is that Thomas's friendship with Sowell endures.

Years later, a former Blackmun law clerk tried to put Blackmun's irritation with Thomas in perspective. Yes, there is a certain collegiality[10] among justices, this person said, but even collegiality has its limitations. "You're in this environment," said the former clerk, "and you have people who are working with you who are, in essence, your enemies."

---

9   **tawdry:** showy but lacking substance
10   **collegiality:** shared respect out of shared power

LEGAL ETHICS

SONIA SOTOMAYOR

Before being appointed to the United States Supreme Court, Sonia Sotomayor served on the next highest level of courts, the Court of Appeals. While in that position, she introduced Supreme Court Justice Antonin Scalia at Hofstra Law School on September 9, 2001. He was giving a speech on legal ethics.

The phrase "legal ethics" brings together two very different terms—law and ethics—and when I think of the phrase, I am reminded of a story that Robert Bork[1] relates in his book *The Tempting of America*. According to the legend, Justice Holmes and Judge Learned Hand, two of the most important legal minds of this century, once had lunch together. Just afterwards, as Holmes began to drive off in his carriage, Hand suddenly ran after him crying, "Do justice, Sir, do justice!" Hearing this plea, Holmes stopped his carriage and retorted: "That is not my job, my job is to apply the law."

What this exchange raises is the degree to which the law is separable from morality, and the degree to which moral insight can either help or hinder one's understandings and applications of the law. Though Justice Holmes and Judge Hand were talking about the kinds of formal legal norms that are passed by Congress or found in the Constitution, the same kind of question can be asked about the less formal norms that guide our professional practice and make up the subject of legal ethics. The question would then involve asking whether legal ethics is completely separable from personal ethics more generally. And if the caliber of mind involved in the exchange between Justice Holmes and Judge Hand is any indication, the question is likely to be a very difficult one, one over which reasonable and highly intelligent persons can disagree.

1　**Robert Bork:** a law professor who was nominated for the Supreme Court in 1987 but not approved by the Senate

Justice Sonia Sotomayor (right) is shaking hands with President Barack Obama (left), who nominated her to a seat on the Supreme Court in 2009. She was confirmed and began to serve later that year. In the middle behind them is Justice Antonin Scalia.

I would never attempt to resolve such a debate here. I would, however, like to say some things that will help clarify the relation, so as to set the stage for Justice Scalia's talk and for some of the kinds of questions that we will need to think about at this conference and that we should grapple with and think about throughout our professional legal careers.

In one sense, legal ethics *is* different from ethics. Ethics is concerned with the norms of conduct that should govern the people *just insofar as they are people,* whereas legal ethics—much like the ethics of many other professional fields—is concerned with the norms that should govern people insofar as they inhabit certain particularized roles, such as those of the lawyer or the judge. An understanding of these rules, and of the ways in which they might be improved, will thus require developing a secondary understanding of how these roles differ, and how they fit together into a larger social practice.

One must also try to understand how these practices might themselves be justified—a question that goes beyond acceptance of the norms. Thus—to use an example that might help clarify these issues—you might come to believe that it is perfectly appropriate for a lawyer working in an adversarial[2] system to zealously[3] advocate for his or her client's rights, if you believe that an adversarial system can produce something of value or truth. Still, it might be inappropriate for a judge in such a system to take one person's side in a controversy, before the case has been heard. Different roles require different norms—as this example shows.

There is, finally, a third dimension to legal ethics, which touches on ethics in a more straightforward sense but still comprises a distinct subject. Legal ethics should provide a person with the professional guidance as how to resolve conflicts when professional norms tell one to conduct oneself in a manner that is somehow at odds with your personal moral views. This might happen, for example, if you are asked to help provide access to justice to an indigent client whose actions you find morally repugnant.

I have now said enough to begin indicating why I view much of Justice Scalia's work as bearing on the topic of legal ethics. Justice Scalia has helped provoke a number of illuminating debates concerning the professional norms that should govern not practicing lawyers—the ordinary topic of legal ethics—but federal judges. I understand Justice Scalia's jurisprudence[4] to begin with a proposition that we should all agree to—namely, that judges should try to interpret the law correctly, and without personal or political bias. He has, however, become one of the most important and outspoken proponents of the idea that following this norm requires the adoption of a particular interpretive methodology, namely that of formalism[5] and plain meaning. Due to the force with which he has presented these ideas, these are terms that have become almost synonymous[6] with his jurisprudence. Justice Scalia has also been uncommonly articulate about how he views this norm as related to the role that federal judges should play in the larger social practice of democratic government. He has argued, in effect, that because federal judges work in a democratic system, they should refrain from reading the Constitution in a way that will remove questions from majoritarian

---

2 **adversarial:** relating to an opponent or a rival
3 **zealously:** with intensity or enthusiasm
4 **jurisprudence:** a philosophy of law
5 **formalism:** a philosophy that emphasizes the role of the legislature in defining the law
6 **synonymous:** meaning the same

resolution—*unless the Constitution is perfectly clear on the matter.* All of this thinking can be viewed as a kind of colloquy[7] on how federal judges should resolve conflicts between their professional norms and the ordinary norms of ethics. Moreover, although Justice Scalia's views on all of these matters have important antecedents,[8] there is no doubt that he has clarified them, and has helped develop them, in a number of very innovative and illuminating ways.

I do not mean to suggest—and the Justice will be the first to agree with me on this one—that any of these thoughts are uncontroversial. To the contrary: Justice Scalia appears to delight in controversy, and his views have provoked a growing body of responses from not only legal but also academic and popular circles. Many—including some very prominent thinkers such as Ronald Dworkin[9]—have questioned whether Justice Scalia's theories of interpretations are the right ones, and have articulated alternatives. Others have wondered whether general theories of interpretation are even helpful when trying to get the law right. Still others have challenged Justice Scalia's ways of understanding the role of a Constitution in our democracy, and the role that judges should play in preserving our nation's values. Finally, a number of critics have argued that Justice Scalia's particular views of how judges should interpret the law might themselves be a reflection of how well these norms further some of his own personal moral views.

As the common saying goes—it is better to be looked over than overlooked—and responses like these are a tribute to just how important and powerful Justice Scalia's presence has been in our current legal culture. Controversies like these are also healthy. They help raise our awareness of how difficult it can be to identify and navigate the conflicts that we all will inevitably feel at times—as lawyers, as judges, or as justices, in integrating our personal sense of morality with the norms of our profession.

---

7 **colloquy:** a formal conversation
8 **antecedents:** previously stated ideas
9 **Ronald Dworkin:** a contemporary legal scholar

Trust in the Supreme Court

Dahlia Lithwick

Why do people obey courts? Is it only the fear that the police or some other part of the executive branch of government would put them in jail if they disobeyed? One reason people obey courts, even when they disagree with a particular decision, is because they have confidence in the judicial system. How the courts maintain the confidence of the public, then, is important to how well they can exert their power.

Justice John Paul Stevens recently told *Inside E Street*[1] that shortly before he retired last year, he worried that he could be "working beyond the time when I would be able to do the job properly." He further explained that when he had announced his dissent from the bench in the Citizens United case in January 2010, he'd stumbled over his sentences, and was concerned that "maybe I was changing in ways I hadn't recognized." It was the first time, he said, that "I had some trouble articulating what I wanted to say." As the year went on and he turned 90, he decided to retire.

Now he has regrets—sort of. "I may have jumped the gun a little bit" when it came to calling it quits, he told *Inside E Street*. "I'm sure that the way the last year has gone, I would have been perfectly capable of continuing the job." The most striking part of the interview is that Stevens had a sort of informal compact with (now-retired) Justice David Souter, that each would warn the other when it was time to go. When Souter retired in 2009, Stevens said half-jokingly, "I lost my guarantee of someone who told me what to do."

A heated public conversation along similar lines has taken place in recent weeks over Ruth Bader Ginsburg, who at 78 is facing awkward calls from some liberals to step down so that President Obama can appoint her replacement while still in office. "There is no indication that Ginsburg is

---

1 *Inside E Street:* an online publication of the AARP, formerly known as the American Association of Retired Persons

slowing down on the job, even after she underwent surgery two years ago for pancreatic cancer that her doctors said was detected at a very early stage," writes Mark Sherman of the Associated Press. But some liberals, the story says, want her to "put self-interest aside and act for the good of the issues they believe in." Writing for *Bloomberg View,* Stephen L. Carter traces the history of this "creepy passion" that reflects "the insidious hope that the justices one party likes will retire while their side still has the opportunity to replace them." It's not just party zealots who demand that justices step aside to be replaced with younger, hotter models. As Carter reminds us, in 1980 officials in the Jimmy Carter administration evidently pressured Justice Thurgood Marshall to resign before the Senate flipped from Democratic to Republican. An outraged Marshall refused to budge. One of the most important lessons of the "creepy passion" about judges and mental competence is that it's quite clear the justices fear nobody will tell them when they are losing it. Surrounded by young clerks and worshipful staff, the justices are less than confident someone will offer up the unvarnished truth—even when it hurts.

THE SUPREME COURT OF THE UNITED STATES 1983 Franklin McMahon

How does the artist emphasize the power of the Supreme Court?

Trust in Branches of Government					
Branch	1999	2002	2005	2008	2010
Legislative	61	67	60	49	45
Executive	63	72	55	42	61
Judicial	80	75	68	70	76

Source: Gallup, Inc.

Numbers indicate the percentage of people in the survey who said they had either a "great deal" or a "fair amount" of trust in each branch of the federal government. Which branch is most trusted?

All this public hand-wringing over mental competence stands in sharp contrast to the almost complete lack of concern about an equally pressing judicial issue: recusal.[2] While the justices are quite open about discussing their fears of overstaying their welcome on the job, they are loath[3] even to consider questions about whether they have been compromised by financial or personal dealings with parties to the cases pending before the court.

Justice Clarence Thomas has been dogged for at least a year by claims that his wife's work for the opponents of health care reform (and her financial remuneration[4] for that work, which Thomas failed to disclose) raised serious ethical questions about whether he should hear the appeal of the challenge to the law that will inevitably come before the court. (Conservative lawmakers have attempted to manufacture a corresponding conflict of interest on the part of Justice Elena Kagan that seems predicated on the idea that since she recuses herself from everything else, she should keep doing that.) But when called upon to comment on their extracurricular speech-making, conclave-attending,[5] and closed-door talking about unspecified ominous threats to "liberty," the justices are not only silent, but defiant. The appearance of senility seems to be a larger worry than the appearance of impropriety.

Even those who have not been accused of conduct unbecoming to the highest judicial officers in the land leap to the defense of their colleagues when it comes to inappropriate or partisan public behavior. At

---

2　**recusal:** the act of a judge removing himself or herself from deciding a case in which people might suspect they have personal reasons to favor one side

3　**loath:** reluctant

4　**remuneration:** payment in money

5　**conclave:** meeting

the Aspen Ideas Festival last month, both Justice Stephen Breyer and former Justice Sandra Day O'Connor took the position that the judicial recusal questions represent, in Breyer's words, "a false issue." O'Connor assured the audience that "if there's a real question, they'd discuss it with their colleagues." Yet looking at the ways in which the justices have become increasingly polarized, politicized, and outspoken (and Ginsburg has been perhaps most outspoken on the question of outspokenness) there seems to be a widespread agreement on the court that the justices are acting out—and an equally widespread agreement to do nothing whatsoever about it.

Certainly many justices are haunted by memories of colleagues who stayed on the bench long after they had become ineffective. Court scholar David Garrow has described chilling scenes of William O. Douglas,[6] returning to work after a debilitating stroke, "call[ing] people the wrong name and utter[ing] non sequiturs," and falling asleep at oral arguments. Still, it's strange that justices who can be so vigilant and cautious about the possibility of overstaying their time on the bench, and how that affects the credibility and integrity of the court, can be so willfully blind to the ways in which their speeches, relationships, and strong rhetoric sow precisely the same kind of doubt about the court. As my friend Jeff Shesol reminded us recently, the court holds its legitimacy in its own hands. Justices engage in controversial extrajudicial conduct not at their own peril; since they sit for life, the reputation they put at risk is the court's.

There is nobody on the current court who is senile, infirm, or even close. But there seems to be some sense among the justices that they cannot trust their own judgment about when that line is crossed. That is why it's doubly worrisome that there are some sitting justices doing as much damage to the perceived legitimacy of the court off the bench as any senile old man could ever do while on it. Shouldn't they be applying the same self-scrutiny to questions of bias, and the appearance of bias, that they apply to matters of mental competence? Being old is not the same as being judicious. The justices should worry less about the former and more about the latter.

---

6 **William O. Douglas:** a justice on the Supreme Court from 1939 to 1975

WHAT THE *BROWN* DECISION MEANS

JACK BALKIN

In 1954, the Supreme Court issued one of the most dramatic rulings in its history. In the case of Brown v. Board of Education of Topeka, *the Court struck down the long-standing legal principle of "separate but equal" in public education. This meant that states and local communities could no longer require racial segregation in schools. Further, the decision laid the groundwork for ending racial segregation in all areas of public life. Though the ruling was controversial among the public and legal scholars, it was a unanimous decision by the justices.*

In the half century since the Supreme Court's decision, *Brown* has become a beloved legal and a political icon.[1] *Brown* is one of the most famous Supreme Court opinions, better known among the lay public than *Marbury v. Madison,* which confirmed the Supreme Court's power of judicial review, or *McCulloch v. Maryland,* which first offered an expansive interpretation of national powers under the Constitution. Indeed, in terms of sheer name recognition, *Brown* ranks with *Miranda v. Arizona,* whose warnings delivered to criminal suspects appear on every police show, or the abortion case, *Roe v. Wade,* which has been a consistent source of political and legal controversy since it was handed down in 1973.

Even if *Brown* is less well known than *Miranda* or *Roe,* there is no doubt that it is the single most honored opinion in the Supreme Court's corpus. The civil rights policy of the United States in the last half century has been premised on the correctness of *Brown,* even if people often disagree (and disagree heatedly) about what the opinion stands for. No federal judicial nominee, and no mainstream national politician today would dare suggest that *Brown* was wrongly decided. At most they might suggest that the opinion was inartfully written, that it depended too much on social science literature, that it did not go far enough, or that it

---

1 **icon:** something highly respected as a symbol

The headline about the *Brown* decision in the *Memphis World* reads "SEGREGATION IN PUBLIC SCHOOLS OUTLAWED BY U. S. SUPREME COURT."

has been misinterpreted by legal and political actors to promote an unjust political agenda. The use made of *Brown* is often criticized, but the idea of *Brown* remains largely sacred in American political culture.

It was not always thus. In the decade following 1954 the Supreme Court and its opinion in *Brown* were vilified[2] in terms far stronger than many of the attacks leveled against *Roe* and *Miranda*. Even many defenders of the result had little good to say about the opinion, arguing that its overruling of previous precedents was abrupt and unexplained and that its use of social science to demonstrate the harm that segregation imposed on black children was unconvincing. The day after the decision, May 18, 1954, James Reston wrote in the *New York Times* that the Court had rejected "history, philosophy, and custom" in basing its decisions in "the primacy of the general welfare. . . . Relying more on the social scientists than on legal precedents—a procedure often in controversy in the past—the Court insisted on equality of the mind and heart rather than on equal school facilities. . . . The Court's opinion read more like an expert paper on sociology than a Supreme Court opinion."

---

2 **vilified:** treated as evil or dangerous

If the defenders of *Brown* were uneasy, its opponents were positively incensed[3] by the decision. People who accuse the contemporary Supreme Court of abusing its office may forget how deeply *Brown* was resented, especially in the South. In March of 1956, southern senators and congressmen issued a "Southern Manifesto" denouncing *Brown* as a "clear abuse of judicial power," that substituted the Justices' "personal, political, and social ideas for the established law of the land." This proved to be one of the more moderate reactions. Although congressional leaders pledged to "use all lawful means to bring about the reversal of this decision which is contrary to the Constitution," other opponents of the decision were less committed to peaceful legal methods. *Brown* gave rise to the era of "massive resistance" in the South, leading President Eisenhower at one point to call in federal troops to enforce the desegregation order in Arkansas. Yet, by the close of the twentieth century, *Brown* had achieved a special place of honor.

One reason for that special status is that *Brown* fits nicely into a widely held and often repeated story about America and its Constitution. This story has such deep resonance in American culture that we may justly regard it as the country's national narrative. I call this story the Great Progressive Narrative. The Great Progressive Narrative sees America as continually striving for democratic ideals from its founding and eventually realizing democracy through its historical development. According to the Great Progressive Narrative, the Constitution reflects America's deepest ideals, which are gradually realized through historical struggle and acts of great political courage. The basic ideals of America and the American people are good, even if America and Americans sometimes act unjustly, even if people acting in the name of the Constitution sometimes perpetrate terrible injustices. The basic ideals of Americans and their Constitution are promises for the future, promises that the country eventually will live up to, and, in so doing, confirming the country's deep commitments to liberty and equality.

It is easy to see how *Brown* fits into this narrative and confirms its truth: Through years of struggle and a great Civil War, America gradually freed itself from an unjust regime of chattel[4] slavery. The country's failures were redeemed by the Thirteenth, Fourteenth, and Fifteenth Amendments to the Constitution. To be sure, the Civil War was followed

---

3 **incensed:** deeply angered
4 **chattel:** relating to personal property

by retrenchment and the establishment of Jim Crow,[5] which was given official sanction in the 1896 decision in *Plessy v. Ferguson*. Nevertheless, eventually the country redeemed itself once again by overturning that unjust precedent and firmly establishing the principle of racial equality. Seen in this way, *Brown* represents the Good Constitution—the Constitution whose deeper principles and truths were only fitfully and imperfectly realized, rather than the Constitution that protected slavery and Jim Crow. By extension, *Brown* also symbolizes the Good America, rather than the country that slaughtered Native Americans, subordinated women, and enslaved blacks. . . .

Indeed, *Brown* has come to mean much more than an honored symbol of equality. It has also come to symbolize important beliefs about the U.S. Supreme Court and the role of courts generally in American democracy. For many Americans, and particularly American liberals, *Brown* became a symbol of what courts devoted to justice could achieve if they had the necessary will and courage. In this respect, *Brown* represents a sea change in attitudes about the proper role of the judiciary. For the generation before *Brown*, the most important constitutional event was surely the struggle over the constitutionality of the New Deal.[6] Prior to the pivotal year of 1937, the Supreme Court had intermittently used its powers of judicial review to strike down what its critics believe was progressive social legislation. The Court argued that these social and economic regulations violated freedom of contract and went beyond the limited powers of the federal government. The Court's attitude was symbolized by two famous cases. *Lochner v. New York*, which struck down a sixty-hour maximum workweek for the baking industry, and *Hammer v. Dagenhart*, which struck down a national child labor law. These cases symbolized the Court's commitment to use judicial review to protect state's rights and limited government. Indeed the period from roughly 1897 to 1937 is sometimes called the *Lochner* era.

After years of struggle and controversy—including President Franklin D. Roosevelt's failed attempt to pack the Supreme Court with allies favorable to his New Deal policies—these cases were finally overruled in the late 1930s and early 1940s by a new Court staffed with Roosevelt appointees. Many drew the lesson that the great problem of the *Lochner* era had been the Supreme Court's resistance to changing times and its hostility to

---

5   **Jim Crow:** a set of racially discriminatory laws that promoted segregation
6   **New Deal:** program of government actions instituted by Franklin Roosevelt during the
    Great Depression to provide economic relief and reform

democracy. Cases like *Lochner* and *Hammer* were incorrectly decided, so the standard account went, because courts did not recognize that they had only a limited role in a democracy. Judicial displacement[7] of legislative prerogatives[8] was antidemocratic, and, as Alexander Bickel would put it, the Supreme Court was a "countermajoritarian" institution that perpetually needed to restrain itself so as not to overstep its bounds. The new jurisprudence[9] that emerged from the New Deal struggle gave both the federal government and the states broad new powers over the economy; it seemed to vindicate the view that courts should exercise judicial restraint and show proper respect for democratic processes.

Against this background, *Brown* seemed to symbolize a very different set of values and a very different vision of the role of courts in a constitutional democracy. In *Brown* the Court held unconstitutional well-settled and long-established practices of many different states and thousands of localities. It struck down precedents that had stood for well over half a century, all in the name of higher constitutional values. For many members of the New Deal generation, *Brown* was worrisome because it seemed to abandon the new religion of judicial restraint all too easily. But for a later generation of thinkers *Brown's* intervention into the stagnant racial politics of the South was precisely what the Constitution demanded. Judicial restraint under these circumstances was not respect for democracy; it was collaboration with evil and capitulation to moral cowardice. For these thinkers, and for their students as well, *Brown* symbolized the Supreme Court's proper role as the articulator and defender of America's fundamental constitutional values. In *Brown*, the story went, the Court took the lead in advancing justice in the face of injustice.

---

7 **displacement:** the act of taking the place of something else
8 **prerogatives:** rights or privileges
9 **jurisprudence:** a philosophy of law

SUPREME COURTSHIP

CHRISTOPHER BUCKLEY

Since the nine members of the Supreme Court serve for life, the Constitution provides a challenging two-part selection process. The president nominates an individual, and the Senate votes to confirm or reject that person. Since 1789, the Senate has confirmed about three-fourths of nominees. In recent years, debates over nominees have sometimes been bitter, public fights over narrow issues. In the novel Supreme Courtship, *Christopher Buckley provides a humorous look at how senators can defeat a nominee. In this excerpt, President Donald P. Vanderdamp has just nominated a man named Cooney to serve on the Supreme Court. Leading the opposition to Cooney is Senator Dexter Mitchell.*

Nominating someone to the Supreme Court can be hard enough for a popular president. For one at the opposite end of the likability spectrum, it presents a daunting challenge, as well as a delicious opportunity for the chief bouncer at the rope line in front of the Supreme Court entryway: the chairman of the Senate Judiciary Committee.

The current occupant of that powerful chair was a man named Dexter Mitchell, senator from the great state of Connecticut. Dexter Mitchell despised Donald P. Vanderdamp, though he was always careful, in his public statements, to say that he had "the greatest respect" for him. He despised him for a variety—or as they say in Washington, "multiplicity"—of reasons. He despised him because he had vetoed S. 322, a bill Mitchell had sponsored that would have required every helicopter rotor blade in the U.S. military to be made in his home state of Connecticut. And he despised Donald P. Vanderdamp for ignoring his suggestion that he appoint *him* to fill the Brinnin vacancy on the high court. (More about that in due course.)

President Vanderdamp's first nominee to succeed Brinnin was a distinguished appellate judge named Cooney. Enormous care had gone into his selection, knowing that Senator Mitchell's Judiciary Committee was preparing an auto-da-fe[1] that would have made the Spanish Inquisition[2] blush. Cooney was a jurist of impeccable[3] credentials. Indeed, he seemed to have been put on earth precisely for the purpose of one day becoming a justice of the United States Supreme Court.

Senator Mitchell's Judiciary Committee staff investigators were known on Capitol Hill as the Wraith Riders, after the relentless, spectral,[4] horse-mounted pursuers of hobbits in *The Lord of the Rings*. It was said in hushed tones on Capitol Hill that the Wraith Riders could find something on anyone: could make it look like . . . Dr. Albert Schweitzer[5] had conducted ghastly live medical experiments on helpless, unanesthetized African children on behalf of Belgian drug companies.

However, faced with the blemishless Judge Cooney, the Wraith Riders were left to whinny[6] there was nothing with which to hang him, not even an unpaid parking ticket. He was an exemplar[7] of every judicial virtue. Not one of his decisions had been overturned by a higher court. As for his personal life, he was so reasonable and wise that he made Socrates sound like a raving, bipolar crank.

Dig deeper, Senator Mitchell told the Wraith Riders. Or dig your own graves. Off they rode, shrieking.

And so, on day two of the Cooney hearings, Senator Mitchell, smiling pleasantly as usual, began: "Judge Cooney, you are, I take it, familiar with the film *To Kill a Mockingbird*?"[8]

Judge Cooney answered yes, he was pretty sure he'd seen it, back in grade school.

"Is there anything about this that you'd care to . . . *tell* the Committee?"

Judge Cooney looked perplexed. Tell? He wasn't quite sure he understood the question.

Senator Mitchell held up a piece of paper as if mere physical contact with it might forever contaminate his fingers.

---

1 **auto-da-fe:** the public execution of a person for his or her beliefs
2 **Spanish Inquisition:** an agency in Spain that began in the 1500s in order to find and punish religious dissidents
3 **impeccable:** without a flaw
4 **spectral:** ghostly
5 **Dr. Albert Schweitzer:** famous humanitarian doctor who lived from 1875 to 1965
6 **whinny:** the sound made by a horse
7 **exemplar:** ideal example
8 *To Kill a Mockingbird:* a novel and movie about racial justice in the South in the 1930s

"Do you recognize this document?"

Not from this distance, Judge Cooney replied, now thoroughly perplexed.

"Then let me refresh your memory," Senator Mitchell said. The vast audience watching the proceedings held its breath, wondering what radioactive material Senator Mitchell had unearthed to incriminate this spotless nominee. It turned out to be a review of the movie that the twelve-year-old Cooney had written for *The Beaverboard*, his elementary school newspaper. "'*Though the picture is overall OK*,'" Senator Mitchell quoted, "'*it's also kind of boring in other parts.*'"

Senator Mitchell looked up, took off his glasses, paused as if fighting back tears, nodded philosophically, and said, "Tell us, Judge, which parts of *To Kill a Mockingbird* did you find quote-unquote boring?"

In his concluding statement several grueling days later, Senator Mitchell said in a more-in-sadness-than-in-anger tone that he could "not in good conscience bring myself to vote for someone who might well show up at the Court on the first Monday of October wearing not black judicial robes but the white uniform of the Ku Klux Klan."

And that was the end of Judge Cooney. The chairman of the Judiciary Committee issued a statement politely inviting the White House to "send us a nominee we can all agree on."

President Donald P. Vanderdamp . . . swallowed what was left of his pride, and instructed his staff to find another Supreme Court nominee, preferably one who hadn't written movie reviews for his elementary school newspaper.

As a nominee for the Supreme Court, Elena Kagan followed the same strategy as Justices John Roberts, Samuel Alito, and Sonia Sotomayor used in their confirmation hearings. They carefully avoided saying anything that would give senators a justification for voting against them.

RESPONDING TO CLUSTER THREE

HOW DOES THE SUPREME COURT EFFECT CHANGE?

Critical Thinking Skill SUMMARIZING KEY IDEAS

1. Explain how the last sentence in the selection by Alexander Hamilton summarizes his key idea about judicial review.

2. Create a Venn diagram to compare and contrast the point of view toward the Supreme Court expressed by Alexis de Tocqueville and Stephen L. Carter. Write a one-paragraph summary based upon your comparison.

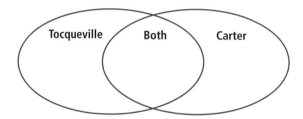

3. The title "Friends and Foes on the Supreme Court" indicates one of the contradictions on the Court. Summarize the selection by describing this and other key contradictions in how the Court operates and how people view it.

4. Select one or two sentences from the selection by Sonia Sotomayor that you think best summarize her key idea. Explain your choice.

5. Compare and contrast the key ideas expressed by Jack Balkin and by Dahlia Lithwick about the role of public opinion in determining the power of the Supreme Court.

6. How does *Supreme Courtship* use references to the classic novel *To Kill a Mockingbird* to satirize the process of evaluating Supreme Court nominees?

Writing Activity: Summarize a Court Ruling

Research a recent Supreme Court ruling, including the facts of the case and the majority and minority opinions of the justices. Then write an article summarizing and explaining the ruling.

A Strong Summary

- contains the main ideas

- includes key supporting details

- organizes information in a clear order

CLUSTER FOUR

THINKING ON YOUR OWN

Critical Thinking Skill
INTEGRATING SOURCES OF INFORMATION

Song of the Powers

David Mason

The game rock-paper-scissors can be traced back to similar games played in China approximately two thousand years ago. In it, each of the three elements has certain powers. Each one can defeat one of the other elements. However, no element has ultimate power. The federal government under the United States Constitution is similar. Each of the three branches has some power, but no single branch is all-powerful. In contests among them, each branch sometimes wins. In the poem below, consider whether the ending suggests a lesson for the three branches of government.

Mine, said the stone,
mine is the hour.
I crush the scissors,
such is my power.
Stronger than wishes,
my power, alone.

Mine, said the paper,
mine are the words
that smother the stone
with imagined birds,
reams of them, flown
from the mind of the shaper.

Mine, said the scissors,
mine all the knives
gashing through paper's
ethereal lives;
nothing's so proper
as tattering wishes.

As stone crushes scissors,
as paper snuffs stone
and scissors cut paper,
all end alone.
So heap up your paper
and scissor your wishes
and uproot the stone
from the top of the hill.
They all end alone
as you will, you will.

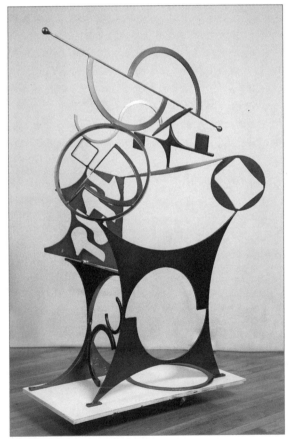

SYMPHONY 2001 James Travers

Like this sculpture, the United States government consists of
interconnected parts that are carefully balanced with each other.

WHY CONGRESS DESERVES AN "A"

SHANKAR VEDANTAM

The rest of the selections in this cluster are presented as paired readings that address the balance of power among the branches of the federal government. The first pair of readings examines the performance of Congress. In the summer of 2011, Congress was deadlocked over whether to raise the debt ceiling, the amount of money the government could legally borrow. In previous years, this had usually been an uncontroversial action to allow the government to pay its bills. However, this time it started a fierce debate about the size of the federal government. As the debate continued, public approval of Congress fell to historic lows. By November 2011, one poll showed that only 9 percent of the population approved of Congress. Shankar Vedantam was among the defenders of Congress.

Stroll around Washington, D.C., this summer, and you will see hordes of tourists thronging the national Mall. Parents ask their kids, "What's the role of Congress?" And the teenagers respond, "The purpose of Congress is to pass laws."

Most people who hear that nowadays feel an urge to laugh. Sure, that's the purpose of Congress, but that isn't what Congress actually *does*. Congress in theory is decisive, but Congress in practice is dysfunctional.[1] If Congress were a student and its handling of the debt-ceiling crisis were an exam, it would get an F, if not expulsion or a referral to the juvenile justice system.

But what if the civics-textbook definition of Congress is wrong? What if Congress is working precisely as designed?

Suppose the purpose of Congress is not to pass laws but to stymie[2] the passage of laws. To be precise, what if the purpose of Congress is to

---

1 **dysfunctional:** not working properly
2 **stymie:** slow down or stop

provide us with maximum theater while delivering the least number of new laws? In this alternate universe, we should expect a congressional landscape littered with good initiatives that have gone nowhere. Check. We should expect to see ideologues on both sides deeply disappointed that after all the time and effort they spend campaigning and winning elections, so little of what they want actually happens. Check. We'd expect that the issues on which Congress is decisive are mostly empty and *symbolic*. Check again.

If the conventional definition of Congress is correct, the only way to explain why Congress accomplishes so little is to assert—as articles, pundits, and analyses have done—that the men and women who happen to be in Congress today are particularly incompetent, unpatriotic, and self-serving.

This is the hidden brain at work. Our minds link actions with intentions. When we see dysfunction and inaction, we ascribe them to *intentional* dysfunction and inaction, rather than to structural factors *designed* to produce inaction.

"I PREFER TO CALL IT THE SYSTEM OF CHECKS AND BALANCES IN ACTION, SENATOR, NOT GRIDLOCK."

How does the system of checks and balances influence how people view Congress?

The idea that Congress is dysfunctional by design is neither original nor new. Political scientists have made this argument for years, but we have ignored it, perhaps because it interferes with our enjoyment of the theater of Congress. If one were to announce, before the play begins, that precisely nothing will happen by the time the curtain drops, it's hard to get the audience engaged.

Here's why Congress is ineffectual by design.

First, most congressional seats are safe seats. Every decade, the two major parties take turns making those seats even safer through gerrymandering.[3] The Republicans, who won big in 2010, now control the lion's share of state legislatures and governorships. They plan to make safe conservative seats safer and swing seats safely conservative. The net result is that in much of the country, the outcomes of general elections are largely decided in primaries. Whoever wins the Republican primary in a safe Republican district wins the general election. Same goes for safely Democratic seats. The voters who really matter are those who vote in primaries—and the most reliable primary voters are hard-liners.

When it comes time to pass legislation, the hard-line politicians these hard-line voters elect can usually undermine moderates in their own parties, making centrist coalitions unstable. When Americans look at congressional dysfunction with disbelief, they are assuming that members of Congress share their moderate political views. They don't. Members of Congress aren't answerable to all their constituents. They are answerable to *hard-liners* in their party primaries, and these hardliners see any attempt to compromise as "caving in." Stanford University political scientist David Brady, who runs a fellowship program I've attended, once found that the more members of Congress vote with their parties, the *less* likely they are to be re-elected.

Second, there's the Senate. Nearly *half* the Senate represent states whose populations together add up to less than the population of California. One half of Congress, in other words, is designed not as a democracy of the people, but a democracy of the states. If 88 percent of the country wants something to happen but the 42 senators who represent the other 12 percent of the country don't want it to happen, it doesn't happen. This has nothing to do with the integrity or competence

---

3 **gerrymandering:** drawing the borders of electoral districts to favor one part or particular candidate

of members of Congress. It's how Congress is designed.

Third, neither party stands for the same issues in all 50 states. It is wildly impractical to expect that country club Republicans in Connecticut will see eye-to-eye with evangelical Republicans in Texas on many issues. Republicans from the 50 states might be members of the same party, but apart from a common name and a handful of issues, many don't share much in common. Expecting Republican or Democratic unity on major issues is like expecting cats to march to the same drummer. Internally divided parties can't ram initiatives into law.

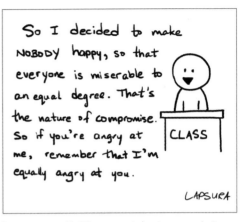

So I decided to make NOBODY happy, so that everyone is miserable to an equal degree. That's the nature of compromise. So if you're angry at me, remember that I'm equally angry at you.

CLASS

LAPSURA

Do you agree with this comment about compromise?

Finally, unlike in countries where major parties raise money en masse and distribute campaign funds to candidates nationwide, most members of Congress raise their own funds. As a result, they aren't beholden to their parties in the way legislators in the United Kingdom are, for example. Even if the national Republican or Democratic party had a unified agenda, it's impossible to impose such agendas on individual members. The parties have limited leverage in getting members of Congress to vote one way or another. Weak, fractured parties, whose members arrive in Congress with their own teams, their own campaign contributors, and their own agendas, have trouble passing laws.

Going back to FDR and even before, presidents have railed against "do-nothing congresses." The astonishing thing is how effective the argument has been for presidents, given that Congress is designed to be dysfunctional.

What we criticize as dysfunction or ineptitude is really an institution designed with a profoundly conservative vision—that's conservative with a small C. Congress is designed to stymie change. You can see this as good or bad, but that's not the point. The point is that it's silly to build a supertanker and then criticize the sailors because the ship doesn't maneuver like a speedboat.

A HOUSE DIVIDED AGAINST ITSELF?

DAVID GERGEN AND MICHAEL ZUCKERMAN

The second reading about the performance of Congress examines how effectively Congress works. Of the three branches of government, Congress is one where the differences among the American public are debated most openly. Members of the judicial branch attempt to stay neutral. Members of the executive branch generally follow the lead of the president. In Congress, though, members stand up for their own constituents and beliefs. David Gergen and Michael Zuckerman consider the impact of these battles on Congress.

When trouble strikes in our personal lives and we are searching for a source, it usually makes sense to take a look in a familiar place—the mirror. And so it should be in our troubled politics today.

Many of us are deeply angry at politicians in Washington and the broken government they have created. We tend to look down upon them as [expletive] and ideologues who are incapable of organizing a two-car funeral. We blame special interests for capturing them, a 24/7 media for encouraging them, and power for corrupting them. Indeed, a list of reasons for broken government could—and will—fill a week of columns.

But perhaps we give too little attention to the basic notion that our politicians are also a reflection of the public they represent. As the old saying goes, we get the president we deserve—and usually the Congress, too. In truth, our fractured politics are due in no small part to a fractured country—one in which consensus and moderation are disappearing. With apologies to President Truman: the buck stops here.

Those of us who are older—born somewhere close to midcentury— grew up in an America where there was a general consensus that the United States was a great nation, that you could be a success if you worked hard and played by the rules, that government had a positive role to play when trouble hit, and that politics must stop at the water's edge as we united against dangerous enemies. But with Vietnam, the tumult of the '60s and '70s, Watergate and more, our sense of common purpose began collapsing.

Listen for a moment to three of the smartest observers in the country who have weighed in this week on the collapse. In this week's *New York Magazine,* columnist Frank Rich argues that by the late 1960s, "the bipartisan national consensus over the central role of government—which had held firm through the Roosevelt, Truman, Eisenhower, Kennedy and Johnson administrations— was kaput. The Reagan revolution was in the wings."

How does this image reinforce the main point that Gergen and Zuckerman are making?

We also began to lose faith in ourselves and our values. In an interview with the *Financial Times* early this week, Professor Michael Porter of the Harvard Business School chimed in with pained observations about what is happening to American competitiveness: "This is shocking for the U.S. If you go back 100 years, you find that the U.S. was a huge pioneer in public education. . . . The U.S. was a real pioneer in creating a national, very deep university system. . . . The U.S. was a pioneer in the interstate highway system. . . . We stepped to the plate in the past and made very, very bold investments in the fundamental environment for competitiveness. But right now, we can't seem to agree on any of these things."

Or listen to William Galston, who was instrumental in helping President Clinton bridge the divides in politics. In *The New Republic,* he argues that the middle is shrinking in politics. In 1992, he points out, Gallup found that 43% of respondents identified themselves as moderates, 37% as conservatives, and 17% as liberals. In 2009, conservatives and liberals were each up 4% and moderates were down by 7%.

Similarly, a study of national election data by Alan Abramovitz found that in 1984, some 41% identified themselves at the midpoint of an ideological scale versus 10% who placed themselves at liberal or conservative extremes. By 2005, the number who identified themselves at the center had dropped to only 28%, while the number at the endpoints had risen to 23%.

We continue to hear that even so, independents have the whip hand in electoral politics and we tend to assume that they are middling in their views, open to argument, and rather homogeneous. But even these assumptions seem doubtful. Frank Rich, for example, highlights a recent Pew survey that suggests that nearly half of independents are actually Democrats (21%) or Republicans (26%) who just shy away from the label, while another 20% are more populist, skeptical Democrats ("Doubting Dems"), 16% are "disaffected" voters with a highly negative view of government, and 17% are "disengaged" altogether. Not exactly a portrait of moderate unity.

Surely there are many sources of the fractures in today's electorate, just as there are many social scientists more qualified to take a crack at explaining them. But one potential contributing factor comes from a fascinating piece in *National Affairs* by Marc Dunkelman, who fears the winnowing out of so-called "middle-tier relationships" for the American citizen.

These relationships have long been, as Dunkelman puts it, "at the root of American community life," and encompass such different-minded acquaintances as "bridge partners, brothers in the Elks club, fellow members of the PTA." But these connections have withered in recent years, even as we stay close to those like-minded folks who inhabit our inner circles of friends and family, and are connected on an unprecedented scale by technology and social media to those farther away. Without these vibrant, heterogeneous "middle-tier" relationships, Dunkelman argues, it may simply be much harder to build the sense of public trust and unity that allows people to stand up to big challenges together.

The good news is that, as with any self-inflicted wound, the power is in our hands to change course. And indeed there is a growing sense in the country that people are finally getting tired of this particularly rancid level of divisiveness. There is a generation rising—singled out in a recent *Time* Magazine cover story as "The Next Greatest Generation"—that, led by its young military veterans, is eager to put aside partisan squabbles to get things done.

The bipartisan group No Labels recently convened a conference call with Starbucks CEO Howard Schultz that they reported drew more than 100,000 participants. And even in Washington itself, Lamar Alexander, a senior Republican senator, recently quit his leadership post so he could devote more time to forging consensus and working across the aisle.

So there is cause for hope. In the meantime, it is up to us to continue to hold those in the halls of power accountable for results and not just party orthodoxy, and to expose ourselves to people outside our handpicked inner sanctums, ideas and opinions outside our own ideologies, and even news sources different from our favorites (unless you're a regular CNN viewer, of course).

Politics in this country has always been rough-and-tumble, and so it should be. But as no less a patriot than former Secretary Bob Gates reminded us last Thursday while accepting the Liberty Medal at the National Constitution Center, "The warning given a long time ago by Benjamin Franklin still applies: 'Either we hang together or we will surely all hang separately.' " That advice likewise applies as much to our representatives in government as it does to those to whom the founders truly entrusted the reins of power—us.

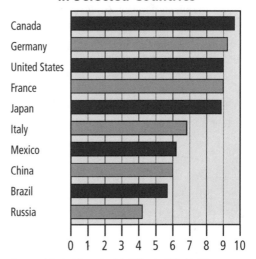

Government Effectiveness in Selected Countries

Canada
Germany
United States
France
Japan
Italy
Mexico
China
Brazil
Russia

0 1 2 3 4 5 6 7 8 9 10

Source: Adapted from the World Bank, "Worldwide Governance Indicators." Data is for 2010.

In the chart above, higher ratings indicate greater effectiveness as measured in a study by the World Bank. Explain whether you think this information supports the point of view of Gergen and Zuckerman.

THE INEVITABILITY OF THE IMPERIAL PRESIDENCY

ERIC A. POSNER

The second pair of readings looks at the power of the presidency. From year to year, executive power increases or decreases depending on the leadership skills of the particular individual serving in the White House. In the following selection, Eric Posner focuses on long-term trends in presidential influence. He wrote this in 2011, while Barack Obama was president.

It is common ground among historians that the presidency has grown and accumulated powers. At the founding, some people expected the presidency to be a ministerial office that would simply put into effect policy chosen by Congress.

George Washington had different ideas, however, and helped set precedents that future presidents would take advantage of. Through most of the 19th century, there were some powerful presidents (notably the early Virginia Dynasty presidents, Jackson, Polk, and Lincoln) but most were junior partners with Congress.

All of this changed in the 20th century. Starting with Theodore Roosevelt, presidents increasingly asserted their right to make and execute policy, especially in the area of foreign affairs and during times of crisis. Franklin Delano Roosevelt enjoyed quasi-dictatorial authority over both the economy during the Great Depression and foreign relations during World War II.

The second half of the 20th century saw the institutionalization of the massive powers claimed by strong presidents like FDR, Theodore Roosevelt, and Lincoln. The budget and staff of the executive branch exploded. For the first time, the United States would have an enormous army permanently stationed around the world during peacetime, and it fell to the president to lead it.

Mount Rushmore in South Dakota shows the faces of four presidents who expanded executive power: George Washington, Thomas Jefferson, Theodore Roosevelt, and Abraham Lincoln.

Meanwhile, the national government took over the regulatory powers that had been exercised by the states. The massive national regulatory apparatus was lodged in the executive branch and was thus, too, put under control of the president.

Congress and the judiciary became increasingly marginal institutions. Congress delegated much of its lawmaking powers to regulatory agencies under the thumb of the president. Courts, too, lost their common law regulatory powers to these agencies. Congress and the courts could react to presidential power in various ways—slowing down projects they disapproved of, adjusting them along the edges—but they could not set policy or block the president's agenda.

To be sure, both institutions retained the formal power to constrain the president. But Congress is a creature of politics, so as people increasingly turned to the president to solve their problems, Congress was forced to go along with the president's agenda.

President Bush went to Congress for counterterrorism authority, but Congress could not deprive him of what he wanted. He, not Congress, set the policy. President Obama has gone to Congress for his financial regulation and health care laws; again, Congress could not say no to him.

And both laws simply give the president various blank checks to regulate.

For most commentators, these trends are matters of significant disquiet.[1] Under the founding design, Congress, not the president, is supposed to make policy; and courts are supposed to enforce the laws that incorporate that policy. The academic effort to reinvigorate the archaic[2] system of checks and balances is fundamentally nostalgic and reactionary. These institutions are as out of place today as the cocked hats and breeches worn by the Founders as they drafted the Constitution.

What has changed? Eighteenth century America was lightly populated, rural, agricultural, and (among the elites who counted) homogenous. Customs and honor counted a lot more for regulation than formal legal institutions did. Dangerous foreign enemies were at a safe distance. Life moved to the slow rhythms of the country lane.

Today, America is huge, diverse, and commercial. Foreign relations are a constant series of crises that must be managed hour-to-hour. The domestic economy is enormously complex, ever-changing, and interconnected. Only one institution can realistically handle these 21st-century challenges, and that is the executive. The presidency has blossomed because Congress, the courts, and the state governments could not handle these challenges as they emerged in the last century.

The major political challenge today is keeping the executive within bounds. But it is no longer possible to rely on Congress and the judiciary to do that. The party system, the media, a communications revolution that has kept the citizenry informed and politically engaged—these institutions are infinitely more important.

---

1 **disquiet:** concern
2 **archaic:** out-of-date

DEFENDING PRESIDENTIAL POWER

CLARENCE THOMAS

The second selection about presidential power is from an opinion written by Supreme Court Justice Clarence Thomas in the case of Hamdi v. Rumsfeld. *Yaser Hamdi was born in Louisiana and raised in Saudi Arabia. In 2001, he was captured in Afghanistan and accused of being an "enemy combatant" who was fighting against the United States military there. According to officials in the executive branch, enemy combatants such as Hamdi could be imprisoned until hostilities were over—an indefinite length of time. Hamdi argued that the Constitution gave him a right to challenge his detention in a court. At the core of the case was the power of the judicial branch to check the power of the executive branch to conduct war. The Supreme Court ruled in Hamdi's favor. This decision preserved the power of judges to review executive branch decisions to detain enemy combatants indefinitely. Thomas dissented. In the following excerpt, citations have been shortened to their name and year.*

The Executive Branch, acting pursuant[1] to the powers vested[2] in the President by the Constitution and with explicit congressional approval, has determined that Yaser Hamdi is an enemy combatant and should be detained. This detention falls squarely within the Federal Government's war powers, and we [the Supreme Court] lack the expertise and capacity to second-guess that decision. As such, petitioners' habeas challenge should fail, and there is no reason to remand[3] the case. The plurality[4] reaches a contrary conclusion by failing adequately to consider basic principles of the constitutional structure as it relates to national security and foreign affairs and by using the balancing scheme of *Mathews v. Eldridge* (1976).

---

1 **pursuant:** according to a set of guidelines
2 **vested:** placed
3 **remand:** to send the case back to a lower court
4 **plurality:** the largest number of judges

Clarence Thomas began serving on the Supreme Court in 1991. A study of justices who had served since 1937 rated him the most consistently conservative member of the court.

I do not think that the Federal Government's war powers can be balanced away by this Court. Arguably, Congress could provide for additional procedural protections, but until it does, we have no right to insist upon them. But even if I were to agree with the general approach the plurality takes, I could not accept the particulars. The plurality utterly fails to account for the Government's compelling interests and for our own institutional inability to weigh competing concerns correctly. I respectfully dissent.

"It is 'obvious and unarguable' that no governmental interest is more compelling than the security of the Nation." *[Haig v. Agee (1981)]* The national security, after all, is the primary responsibility and purpose of the Federal Government. *[Youngstown Sheet & Tube Co. v. Sawyer (1952); The Federalist No. 23].* But because the Founders understood that they could not foresee the myriad[5] potential threats to national security that might later arise, they chose to create a Federal Government that necessarily possesses sufficient power to handle any threat to the security of the Nation. The power to protect the Nation "ought to exist without limitation . . . *[b]ecause it is impossible to foresee or define the extent and variety of national exigencies,[6] or the correspondent extent & variety of the means which may be necessary to satisfy them.* The circumstances that endanger the safety

---

5 **myriad:** large number
6 **exigencies:** conditions that require quick action

of nations are infinite; and for this reason no constitutional shackles[7] can wisely be imposed on the power to which the care of it is committed." *[The Federalist No. 23]*

The Founders intended that the President have primary responsibility—along with the necessary power—to protect the national security and to conduct the Nation's foreign relations. They did so principally because the structural advantages of a unitary Executive[8] are essential in these domains. "Energy in the executive is a leading character in the definition of good government. It is essential to the protection of the community against foreign attacks." *[The Federalist No. 70]* The principle "ingredien[t]" for "energy in the executive" is "unity." *[The Federalist No. 70]* This is because "[d]ecision, activity, secrecy, and dispatch will generally characterise the proceedings of one man, in a much more eminent[9] degree, than the proceedings of any greater number." *[The Federalist No. 70]*

These structural advantages are most important in the national-security and foreign-affairs contexts. "Of all the cares or concerns of government, the direction of war most peculiarly demands those qualities which distinguish the exercise of power by a single hand." *[The Federalist No. 74]* Also for these reasons, John Marshall[10] explained that "[t]he President is the sole organ of the nation in its external relations, and its sole representative with foreign nations." [speech in Congress, (1800)] To this end, the Constitution vests in the President "[t]he executive Power," Art. II, [Section] 1, provides that he "shall be Commander in Chief of the" armed forces, [Section] 2, and places in him the power to recognize foreign governments, [Section] 3.

This Court has long recognized these features and has accordingly held that the President has *constitutional* authority to protect the national security and that this authority carries with it broad discretion.

"If a war be made by invasion of a foreign nation, the President is not only authorized but bound to resist force by force. He does not initiate the war, but is bound to accept the challenge without waiting for any special legislative authority. . . . Whether the President in fulfilling

---

7 **shackles:** things or ideas that limit movement
8 **unitary Executive:** a theory about interpreting the Constitution that gives greater power to the presidency
9 **eminent:** outstanding or noticeable
10 **John Marshall:** a member of Congress from Virginia; he served as the Chief Justice of the Supreme Court from 1801 to 1835

his duties, as Commander in-chief, in suppressing an insurrection,[11] has met with such armed hostile resistance . . . is a question to be decided *by him.*" *[Prize Cases (1863)]*

The Court has acknowledged that the President has the authority to "employ [the Nation's Armed Forces] in the manner he may deem most effectual to harass and conquer and subdue the enemy." *[Fleming v. Page (1850)]* With respect to foreign affairs as well, the Court has recognized the President's independent authority and need to be free from interference. See, e.g.,[12] *United States v. Curtiss-Wright Export Corp. (1936)* (explaining that the President "has his confidential sources of information. He has his agents in the form of diplomatic, consular and other officials. Secrecy in respect of information gathered by them may be highly necessary, and the premature disclosure of it productive of harmful results"). *[Chicago & Southern Air Lines, Inc. v. Waterman S. S. Corp. (1948)]*

Congress, to be sure, has a substantial and essential role in both foreign affairs and national security. But it is crucial to recognize that *judicial* interference in these domains destroys the purpose of vesting

The Supreme Court decides what is right and what is wrong according to the Constitution. No higher court exists in the United States. Justice Robert Jackson, who served on the Court from 1941 to 1954, once quipped, "We are not final because we are infallible [always correct], we are infallible because we are final."

---

11 **insurrection:** rebellion or upheaval
12 **e.g.:** for example

primary responsibility in a unitary Executive. I cannot improve on Justice Jackson's[13] words, speaking for the Court:

"The President, both as Commander-in-Chief and as the Nation's organ[14] for foreign affairs, has available intelligence services whose reports are not and ought not to be published to the world. It would be intolerable that courts, without the relevant information, should review and perhaps nullify actions of the Executive taken on information properly held secret. Nor can courts sit *in camera*[15] in order to be taken into executive confidences. But even if courts could require full disclosure, the very nature of executive decisions as to foreign policy is political, not judicial. Such decisions are wholly confided by our Constitution to the political departments of the government, Executive and Legislative. They are delicate, complex, and involve large elements of prophecy. They are and should be undertaken only by those directly responsible to the people whose welfare they advance or imperil. They are decisions of a kind for which the Judiciary has neither aptitude, facilities nor responsibility and which has long been held to belong in the domain of political power not subject to judicial intrusion or inquiry." *[Chicago & Southern Air Lines, Inc. v. Waterman S. S. Corp. (1948)]*

Several points, made forcefully by Justice Jackson, are worth emphasizing. First, with respect to certain decisions relating to national security and foreign affairs, the courts simply lack the relevant information and expertise to second-guess determinations made by the President based on information properly withheld. Second, even if the courts could compel the Executive to produce the necessary information, such decisions are simply not amenable to judicial determination because "[t]hey are delicate, complex, and involve large elements of prophecy." . . . Third, the Court in *Chicago & Southern Air Lines* and elsewhere has correctly recognized the primacy of the political branches in the foreign-affairs and national-security contexts.

For these institutional reasons and because "Congress cannot anticipate and legislate with regard to every possible action the President may find it necessary to take or every possible situation in which he might act," it should come as no surprise that "[s]uch failure of Congress . . . does not, 'especially . . . in the areas of foreign policy and national

---

13 **Justice Jackson:** Robert Jackson, who served on the Supreme Court from 1941 to 1954
14 **organ:** body or agency
15 **camera:** the chamber of a judge

security,' imply 'congressional disapproval' of action taken by the Executive." *[Dames & Moore v. Regan (1981)]* Rather, in these domains, the fact that Congress has provided the President with broad authorities does not imply—and the Judicial Branch should not infer—that Congress intended to deprive him of particular powers not specifically enumerated. *[Dames & Moore v. Regan (1981)]* As far as the courts are concerned, "the enactment of legislation closely related to the question of the President's authority in a particular case which evinces[16] legislative intent to accord the President broad discretion may be considered to 'invite' 'measures on independent presidential responsibility.'" *[Dames & Moore v. Regan (1981)]*

Finally, and again for the same reasons, where "the President acts pursuant to an express or implied authorization from Congress, he exercises not only his powers but also those delegated by Congress[, and i]n such a case the executive action 'would be supported by the strongest of presumptions and the widest latitude of judicial interpretation, and the burden of persuasion would rest heavily upon any who might attack it.'" *[Dames & Moore v. Regan (1981)]*. That is why the Court has explained, in a case analogous[17] to this one, that "the detention[,] ordered by the President in the declared exercise of his powers as Commander in Chief of the Army in time of war and of grave public danger[, is] not to be set aside by the courts without the clear conviction that [it is] in conflict with the Constitution or laws of Congress constitutionally enacted." *[Ex parte Quirin (1942)]* This deference extends to the President's determination of all the factual predicates[18] necessary to conclude that a given action is appropriate. *[Ex parte Quirin (1942)]*

---

16 **evinces:** shows
17 **analogous:** similar in basic ways
18 **predicates:** bases

THE SWORD AND THE ROBE

THURGOOD MARSHALL

The third pair of readings focuses on judicial power. The Founders gave Supreme Court justices lifetime terms in order to protect them from political influences. Yet justices are not separate from the world they live in. This excerpt is from a speech delivered in 1981 by Justice Thurgood Marshall to a group of federal district court judges.

Well, you win a few and you lose a few. It's in the nature of the process that you can't always be on the winning side. This term the Court has faced a number of difficult questions, and unfortunately, we have been sharply divided over many of them. Of course, we have it a little easier than you do.

When you [judges on a lower court] face a tough issue, you might struggle with it, then finally say, "Well, that's our decision. Let the Supreme Court reverse us if we are wrong." We've found a better method for dealing with the tough ones. We can say, "That's our decision. Let the lower courts figure it out. After all, isn't that what they're for?"

And it's true. Much of the work of any federal judge involves trying to decipher[1] and to apply the sometimes conflicting messages contained in the cases we decide. Often our opinions seem unclear. I can only assure you that we do the best we can. If our opinions sometimes seem to offer little guidance, bear in mind that we try to decide only the case before us. The structure of the law is built that way, case by case, and all of us judges are constrained to work within that framework. Sudden and sweeping changes in the law must come from other branches of government. We as judges are not in a position to dictate policy; we can only interpret the Constitution and the laws of the land, determining what they permit, what they require, and what they forbid.

---

1 **decipher:** interpret, particularly by breaking a code

This task of interpretation is the cornerstone of the judicial process. As we undertake it, we must strive for neutrality. None of us is perfect, and I recognize that neutrality is more ideal than real. Each of us brings along to the judicial role certain preconceived biases. It is, I suppose, impossible to make a decision totally uninfluenced by them. But we as judges must try to do so to the extent we possibly can.

This ideal of neutrality is particularly hard to maintain in times such as these, when our society faces major unsolved problems. Indeed we judges are frequently criticized these days for our neutrality. For example, it is argued by some members of our society that the judiciary has not taken an active enough role in combating crime. It is urged that we, as judges, should take sides, that we should stand shoulder to shoulder with the police and prosecutors. Convictions should be easier, appellate review more rapid, and resort to habeas corpus[2]—what the Founders of this Republic called the Great Writ—drastically curtailed. All of this frightens me because when I was in law school, I was taught not that judges were there to see the defendant convicted and punished in every case, but that they were there to see justice done in every case. *Of course*

Marshall believed that "the structure of the law is built . . . case by case." These cases work together to create the legal climate in the country.

---

2 **habeas corpus:** the legal requirement that prevents the government from imprisoning a person without a charge

the state had to carry a heavy burden to obtain a conviction. *Of course* appellate judges would weigh each case carefully. *Of course* an individual, once convicted, could attack his sentence later. This, so I was taught, was not to coddle[3] the guilty, but to protect the innocent. I was raised in the days when the prevailing maxim was: "It is better that a thousand guilty people go free than that one innocent person suffer unjustly."

Well, that's just what I was taught, and maybe I was taught wrong. But the suggestion that we as judges take sides frightens me for another, more fundamental reason as well. As I have said, judges are required in our system to be as neutral as they possibly can, to stand above the political questions in which the other branches of government are necessarily entangled. The Constitution established a legislative branch to make the laws and an executive branch to enforce them. Both branches are elected and are designed to respond to ever changing public concerns and problems. Indeed, as we were reminded just last November, the failure of either branch to respond to the will of the majority can quickly be remedied at the polls.

But the Framers of the Constitution recognized that responsiveness to the will of the majority may, if unchecked, become a tyranny of the majority. They therefore created a third branch—the judiciary—to check the actions of the legislature and the executive. In order to fulfill this function, the judiciary was intentionally isolated from the political process and purposely spared the task of dealing with the changing public concerns and problems. Article III judges are guaranteed life tenure. Similarly, their compensation cannot be decreased during their term in office—a provision, as we have recently seen, that certainly has its tangible benefits. Finally, the constitutional task we are assigned as judges is a very narrow one. We cannot make the laws, and it is not our duty to see that they are enforced. We merely interpret them, through the painstaking process of adjudicating[4] actual "cases or controversies" that come before us.

We have seen what happens when the courts have permitted themselves to be moved by prevailing political pressures, and have deferred to the mob rather than interpret the Constitution. *Dred Scott, Plessy, Korematsu* and the trial proceedings in *Moore v. Dempsey* come readily to mind as unfortunate examples. They are decisions of which the

---

3   **coddle:** treat gently
4   **adjudicating:** ruling on

The Founders protected the Supreme Court from direct political pressure. The Supreme Court becomes controversial, though, when a decision goes against a popular point of view.

entire judicial community, even after all these years, should be ashamed. There have also been times when the courts have stood proudly as a bulwark[5] against what was politically expedient but also unconstitutional. One need only recall the school desegregation cases to understand why this ability to stand above the fray is so important.

Our central function is to act as neutral arbiters of disputes that arise under the law. To this end, we bind ourselves through our own code of ethics [to] avoid even the appearance of impropriety or partiality. We must handle the cases that come before us without regard for what the result might meet with public approval. We must decide each case in accordance with the law. We must not reach for a result that we, in our arrogance, believe will further some goal not related to the concrete case before us. And we must treat the litigants in every case in an even-handed manner. It would be as wrong to favor the prosecution in every criminal case as it would be to favor the plaintiff in every tort suit.

We must never forget that the only real source of power that we, as judges, can tap is the respect of the people. We will command that respect only as long as we strive for neutrality. If we are perceived as campaigning for particular policies, as joining with other branches of government in resolving questions not committed to us by the Constitution, we may gain some public acclaim in the short run. In the long run, however, we will cease to be perceived as neutral arbiters, and we will lose that public respect so vital to our function.

---

5 **bulwark:** a barrier against some type of attack

I do not suggest that we as judges should not be concerned about the problem of crime. Every thinking American is worried about it. And just about all of us have, lurking somewhere in the back of our minds, what we consider the ideal solution. But when we accepted the judicial mantle, we yielded our rights to advocate publicly our favored solutions for society's problems. The tools for solving these problems are in the hands of the other branches of government because that is where the Constitution has placed them. That is also where we should leave them. I therefore urge that you politely disregard any suggestion that you give up the robe for the sword.

What does this image suggest about the relationship between members of the judiciary and the public?

WANTED: MORE JUDICIAL ACTIVISM!

JAMES HUFFMAN

The second reading about judicial power focuses on an issue that people have debated since the Constitutional Convention in 1787: judicial activism. Some argue that courts should actively protect liberty by challenging actions by the legislative and executive branches. Others argue that courts can best protect liberty by showing restraint and not expanding government power.

The Institute for Justice (IJ) has released a new study titled, "Government Unchecked: The False Problem of 'Judicial Activism' and the Need for Judicial Engagement." One of the authors, Clark Neily, published a commentary in *The Wall Street Journal* summarizing its findings. According to IJ's accounting, between 1954 and 2003, Congress passed 16,015 laws, only 104 of which were struck down by the Supreme Court. During the same period, state legislatures passed 1,209,075 laws of which 455 were found unconstitutional by the Supreme Court. Rather than paint a picture of judicial activism, the authors conclude that the empirical evidence shows a disengaged judiciary failing to meet its responsibility to protect the liberties of American citizens.

In reaction to the IJ report, Ed Whalen, of *National Review Online,*[1] lamented "that the good folks at the Institute for Justice . . . continue their misguided campaign against the very real problem of 'judicial activism.'" Mr. Whalen's objection is not surprising. It seems that everyone—on both sides of the aisle—loves to hate judicial activism. But the folks at IJ have a point that lovers of liberty, whether on the left or the right, should heed.

---

1   *National Review Online:* the online publication operated by *National Review,* one of the country's leading conservative magazines

Almost twenty years ago I presented a lecture at the Heritage Foundation titled, "A Case for Principled Judicial Activism." For a mid-day lecture, it drew a pretty good crowd. At the conclusion there was polite applause, but my sense was that only Roger Pilon, a constitutional scholar at the Cato Institute, was in enthusiastic agreement with my thesis.

In a nutshell my thesis was that courts in the United States should be restrained in second guessing legislative and administrative policy decisions, but activist in the protection of liberty and the enforcement of constitutional limits on government power. Many at Heritage were sympathetic with my argument for protecting neglected economic liberties, and for confining Congress to its enumerated powers. But most were also admirers of former Attorney General Ed Meese and Judge Robert Bork, both of whom were staunch critics of "judicial activism." With Mr. Meese being a resident scholar at Heritage, it seems that few, if any there, had had the temerity[2] to make a case for judicial activism—even if principled.

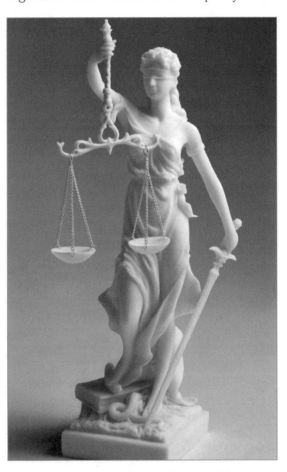

Artists have created many sculptures and paintings of the figure known as Lady Justice. What do you think her blindfold, scales, and sword symbolize?

In the 1980s, conservative objections to judicial activism were rooted in the legacy of the Warren Court. Of course *Roe v. Wade,*[3] with its unwritten right of privacy, was the poster child of judicial activism, but

---

2 **temerity:** courage
3 ***Roe v. Wade:*** the 1973 Supreme Court decision that struck down many state laws against abortion

numerous Supreme Court decisions proclaiming the rights of the accused also ran counter to the conservatives' law and order agenda for government.

Today, objections to judicial activism are more likely to come from the left. *Citizens United v. Federal Election Commission* (invalidating, as a violation of the First Amendment, a prohibition on "electioneering communication" by corporations and unions) is condemned for overriding the will of the majority. The possibility of a Supreme Court invalidation of the individual mandate provision of the Patient Protection and Affordable Care Act has liberal commentators sharpening their pencils to attack judicial activism from the Court's conservative wing, should the law be found unconstitutional.

From a political perspective, it is not surprising that conservatives and liberals are selective in their condemnation of Supreme Court decisions as judicial activism. In a pragmatic world of whatever-it-takes politics, it would be foolhardy to neglect the courts in advancing one's agenda. But having done so, it is a bit unseemly to then appeal to higher principle when the courts advance the other side's political agenda.

What does this cartoon suggest about the phrase "judicial activist"?

The objection to judicial activism is an appeal to higher principles, albeit with mistaken understandings of those principles as they are embedded in the United States Constitution. One principle said to be violated by an activist court is separation of powers. A second is popular sovereignty.

It is said that judicial invalidation of legislative enactments breeches the wall of separation between the three branches of government. But as James Madison wrote in *Federalist* No. 48, "unless these departments be so far connected and blended, as to give to each a constitutional control over the others, the degree of separation which the maxim requires as essential to a free government, can never in practice, be duly maintained." In other words, if each branch of government is checked only by itself, there is no check at all.

It falls to the courts, as Chief Justice John Marshall argued in *Marbury v. Madison*, to decide cases within their jurisdiction, a responsibility requiring the courts to determine what the law is, including the law of the Constitution. The rule of law requires nothing less. Congress' powers are enumerated in the Constitution to protect against the tendency of government officials, even when democratically elected, to aggregate power to themselves. If in a case properly before the courts, judges have no authority to interpret and enforce the constitutional limitations on Congressional authority, leaving it to Congress to determine those limits, the only real limits will be political. A century of judicial deference to Congressional determination of its own constitutional powers (reflected in the IJ study's data for the last half century) is testimony to the necessity of active judicial enforcement of the law of the Constitution.

The objection that judicial invalidation of legislative enactments violates the principle of popular sovereignty reflects a fundamental misunderstanding of the relationship between popular sovereignty and democracy, and of the role of democracy under the United States Constitution.

Sovereignty speaks to political power. He, or they, who are sovereign have power. Popular sovereignty derives from liberty—from a rejection of the claim that political power is acquired by force, endowed by divinities, or inherited by lineal descent. Individuals are sovereign unto themselves, but social action is seldom possible under a rule of unanimity respectful of each individual's sovereignty. So for pragmatic reasons, we settle for majority rule. It is the best we can do in an imperfect world. It is, as Professor Martin Diamond once concluded, the least worst form of government. It is the form of government most likely to be respectful of liberty.

There is no principled argument for democracy beyond that deriving from liberty. Democracy allows individuals a say in social actions affecting them. The registering of a vote is an exercise of individual liberty. What is the principle, independent of liberty, which justifies social decisions by a simple majority? Is there any basis for believing that social decisions arrived at by a majority of all adults will better serve the society than decisions arrived at by a majority of all male adults, or all property owners, or by an elite corps of highly trained experts, or even by a benevolent dictator? Our objection to the latter alternatives is that individuals are excluded from decisions affecting them, not that a decision reached by a majority of all adults will be better in some principled sense. It may be true that tyranny by a majority will burden the liberty of fewer individuals than tyranny by a monarch or dictator, but it is tyranny nonetheless.

Democratic government is not the end of the Constitution. It is one of several means, as is the separation of powers, proposed by the Framers to achieve the end stated in the Declaration of Independence: "Governments are instituted among Men" "to secure" the "unalienable Rights" of "all Men." The words are reordered, but the meaning is clear. Government exists, first and foremost, to protect liberty—to protect liberty from the depredations[4] of other individuals acting alone and in concert.

The Framers of the United States Constitution understood that liberty can be denied as well, or even more effectively, by individuals acting in concert through government as by individuals and groups acting outside the law. In Federalist No. 10, James Madison urged that "a republic . . . offers the cure" for the threat of tyranny of the majority.

But Madison knew that more than a republican form of government was required to safeguard liberty. In Federalist No. 16, he wrote that the success "of a constitution in any degree competent to its own defence, and of a people enlightened enough to distinguish between a legal exercise and an illegal usurpation of authority . . . would require not merely a factious majority in the legislature, but the concurrence of the courts of justice, and of the body of the people."

---

4 **depradations:** attacks

Alexander Hamilton was even more to the point in Federalist No. 78 where he wrote that limitations on legislative authority and affirmative guarantees of liberty "can be preserved in practice no other way than through the medium of the courts of justice; whose duty it must be to declare all acts contrary to the manifest tenor of the constitution void. Without this, all the reservations of the particular rights or privileges would amount to nothing."

A fear of judges who would legislate from the bench is not unwarranted. It happens. But the rogue[5] judge is far more easily restrained than is the legislative majority or the executive official acting in service to powerful political interests at the expense of individual liberty. The appellate process effectively constrains most abuses of judicial power. The only court that is unchecked by the prospect of appeal is the Supreme Court, and the IJ data shows a very low level of Supreme Court activism, understood as the invalidating of legislative actions.

One does not need a study to confirm that state and federal laws and regulations that restrict liberty have multiplied since the New Deal. Nor is a study necessary to confirm that the Supreme Court has been selective in its enforcement of constitutional liberties. The Court has expressly relied on a false distinction between civil and economic liberties, with the latter given far less scrutiny than the former. While the Court explains its restraint with respect to burdens on economic liberties in terms of deference to Congress and to agency expertise, there is absolutely no basis in the Constitution for such a hierarchy of rights.

In light of its mission to seek judicial enforcement of economic liberties, the Institute for Justice's interest in greater judicial engagement is not surprising. What is surprising, and unfortunate for liberty, is that most advocates of constitutional rights, on both the political left and right, seek judicial action when it serves their constituency, but deride it when the rights of others are at stake.

---

5 **rogue:** uncontrolled or without principle

RESPONDING TO CLUSTER FOUR

THINKING ON YOUR OWN

Critical Thinking Skill INTEGRATING SOURCES OF INFORMATION

1. Explain the line "They all end alone" from the poem by David Mason. How might this idea apply to the interaction of the three branches of government?

2. Summarize why Shankar Vedantam believes that Congress is ineffectual by design. Use other selections from this book, current events, or your knowledge to explain why you think his evidence is valid or not.

3. Use a chart like the one below to analyze how David Gergen and Michael Zuckerman integrate information from other sources to support their main idea.

Source of Information	Summary
Author's Main Idea	

4. Compare and contrast the points of view of Eric Posner and Clarence Thomas toward the power of the executive branch. Then integrate information from both sources as you write a summary of your own opinion about presidential power.

5. Explain whether you agree with either Thurgood Marshall or James Huffman about the proper role of courts. In your explanation, cite specific examples from each writer.

Writing Activity: Integrate Sources in an Argument

Using at least four of the selections in this cluster, write a one- to two-page answer to this question: Which branch of government has the most influence today?

A Strong Argument

- makes a clear claim (states an opinion) in the first paragraph

- supports the claim with facts, examples, or reasons

- cites specific comments by at least three writers in this cluster

- presents a conclusion that summarizes the main points

CLOSE READING

Re-reading, we find a new book. —Mason Cooley

Close reading is the careful interpretation of a text. Re-reading is the key strategy for close reading. The "new book" readers often encounter on re-reading is layered with meaning.

There is no single right way to do a close reading of a text. The following general process, however, presents three broad stages or levels in re-reading that build on one another to help produce a deep understanding of a text.

1. First Readings: Build Understanding

On a first reading, focus on grasping the literal or explicit meaning of a text. Answer the questions as you read, paraphrase key ideas, and jot down any questions you have.

Informational Text	
Questions to Ask	**Where to Look for Answers**
What is the main idea?	Title, introduction, or first few paragraphs
What information backs up the main idea?	Body paragraphs, especially their topic sentences
How are the ideas in the text related to one another?	Transitions between sections/ideas
What conclusion does the writer draw, and how does it relate to the main idea and supporting ideas?	Concluding paragraphs

Argumentative Text	
Questions to Ask	**Where to Look for Answers**
What is the main claim, or point the writer is trying to prove?	Title, introduction, or first few paragraphs
What evidence does the writer provide to back up that claim?	Body paragraphs, especially their topic sentences
What counterclaims, if any, does the writer address?	Body paragraphs, often marked with such words and phrases as "in contrast," "despite," "while it is true that"
How are the ideas in the text related to one another?	Transitions between sections/ideas
What conclusion does the writer draw, and how does it relate to the main claim and supporting ideas?	Concluding paragraphs

Narrative Text	
Questions to Ask	**Where to Look for Answers**
What event starts the narrative in motion?	Introduction or first few paragraphs
What is the setting of the narrative?	Introduction and throughout
Who are the people or characters in the narrative?	Introduction and throughout
What problem do the people or characters face?	Introduction and throughout
What happens to the people or characters as the narrative unfolds?	Body paragraphs
What is the outcome or resolution of the narrative?	Concluding paragraphs

Poetry	
Questions to Ask	**Where to Look for Answers**
If the poem tells a story, what is the basic outline of that story?	Throughout
What is the tone of the poem?	Throughout
What images, words, or ideas stand out as striking?	Throughout
What images, words, or ideas are repeated, if any?	Throughout
What message do you see in the poem?	Title, throughout

2. Focused Re-readings: Analyze the Text and Gather Evidence

Re-reading after you have grasped a basic understanding of a text is the stage at which you are most likely to encounter that "new book" referred to in the beginning quote, because at this level you analyze the text carefully and focus on details that may bring new meaning to what you have read. The chart below shows some of the points you can focus on in a re-reading of almost any kind of text. It also shows what questions you can ask and where and how you can discover the answers to those questions.

Focused Re-reading		
Focus and Thinking Skills	**Questions to Ask**	**Finding Textual Evidence**
Author's purpose, such as to inform, put forward an argument, entertain, satirize, tell a story *Thinking skills: Recognize explicit statements; draw inferences about implied purpose(s)*	Why did the writer write this? Is the purpose stated explicitly or is it only implied?	Look in the title and beginning paragraphs for quotes that show the answers to your questions.

continued

Focused Re-reading *(cont.)*		
Focus and Thinking Skills	**Questions to Ask**	**Finding Textual Evidence**
Word choice and style, including length of sentences, variety of sentence beginnings, and variety of sentence types *Thinking skills: Analyze; break passages down by word choice and sentence style and look for patterns*	What words and phrases caught your attention for their strength and clarity? Does the author tend to use long sentences, short sentences, or a variety of sentence lengths? Do the sentences begin in a variety of ways (for example, subject first, prepositional phrase first, etc.)?	Look throughout for examples that demonstrate the results of your analysis (for example, three vivid word choices, three varied sentence patterns, etc.). In a long text, examine a section from the beginning, two or three sections from the middle, and a section from the end.
Figurative language, such as similes, metaphors, hyperbole, alliteration *Thinking skills: Analyze to identify figures of speech; classify the type of figurative language; compare figurative language to a possible replacement in literal language*	What figures of speech does the writer use? What do they accomplish that literal language would not?	Look throughout, but especially in descriptive passages, for various examples of figurative language and compare them to literal language.
Structure, including main sections and such organizational patterns as chronological order and order of importance *Thinking skills: Analyze to identify the sections of a text; classify to determine the organizational pattern*	What are the main sections of the text? What is the organizational pattern of the text?	Look throughout the text for transitional words and phrases that show both where sections break and how they are connected. Identify the main ideas from each section.
Point of view in fiction, including choice of narrator *Thinking skills: Analyze narrative to identify point of view; compare points of view by imagining a passage told from a different point of view and evaluating the effect.*	Is the story told from the first- or third-person point of view? If it is not in first-person, how much does the narrator know about the characters? What effect does the choice of narrative point of view have on the text? Why might the author have chosen that point of view?	Look for pronouns. If the narrator refers to himself or herself as "I," the story is in first-person. Look at key passages in which important information is revealed for examples that show the effect of point of view on the narrative.

continued

Focused Re-reading (cont.)		
Focus and Thinking Skills	**Questions to Ask**	**Finding Textual Evidence**
Point of view in nonfiction, including frame of reference, such as scientist, parent, teenager *Thinking skills: Recognize explicit statements; draw inferences about the writer from telling details*	What is the writer's frame of reference?	Look in the introduction and body paragraphs for details that give insight into the writer's experience, worldview, and possible bias.
Implied meanings *Thinking skills: Analyze details; draw inferences and conclusions*	What is left unsaid? What inference can you draw from a collection of details when you "read between the lines"?	Look throughout for details that "show" not "tell." In fiction these would include the actions of the characters and details of the setting. In nonfiction, these might appear in descriptive passages where the reader is left to draw his or her own conclusions. Find examples that support your interpretation of the implied meaning.

Different kinds of texts suggest additional points to focus on during re-reading.

Focused Re-Reading of Informational and Argumentative Text		
Focus and Thinking Skills	**Questions to Ask**	**Finding Textual Evidence**
Clarification and verification of information *Thinking skills: Define key terms; analyze complicated sentences and paragraphs; compare to other sources to verify information*	What parts confused you? What did you not understand well on first reading? What seemed to contradict information you thought you knew?	Look in passages that raised questions in your mind in first reading; refer to outside sources if necessary for confirming or contradicting information.
Assumptions *Thinking skills: Logical thinking to evaluate the assumption underlying the claim*	Does every claim depend on a valid assumption?	Look for passages that put forward claims in an argument; look for examples, if any, of hidden assumptions.

continued

Focused Re-Reading of Informational and Argumentative Text (cont.)		
Focus and Thinking Skills	**Questions to Ask**	**Finding Textual Evidence**
Development of an argument and key supporting ideas *Thinking skills: Evaluate the relevance, sufficiency, and importance of the supporting details; distinguish fact from opinion*	By what method does the writer attempt to prove his or her point? Are the supporting ideas relevant and sufficient to prove the point?	Look throughout for all the facts, reasons, and examples offered in support of each claim and/or counterclaim.
Style and tone *Thinking skills: Analyze language choices; evaluate appropriateness*	Is the style formal and respectful, or informal and full of "loaded" language (words that carry strong, usually negative connotations)?	Look throughout, but especially at the beginning and ending where the author wants to make his or her point most strongly, for examples that show formal, respectful language or disrespectful loaded language.

Focused Re-reading of Fiction and Drama		
Focus and Thinking Skills	**Questions to Ask**	**Finding Textual Evidence**
Plot *Thinking skills: Sequence; draw inferences; examine cause-effect relationships*	What is the impact of each main development of the plot on the characters?	Look for examples of characters' words or actions before a turning point in the story and after a turning point.
Setting *Thinking skills: Draw inferences*	How does the setting contribute to the mood of the story? How do the details of the setting help define characters?	Look for descriptive details throughout the story about the time and physical characteristics of the place of the events and their impact on mood and characters.
Characters *Thinking skills: Analyze details of characterization; generalize from details; draw inferences from details*	How does each character contribute to the development of the plot? How do the details of characterization and the dialogue reveal the characters' personalities and motivations? Why do characters act as they do?	Look throughout for character 1) descriptions, 2) thoughts, 3) words, 4) actions, 5) changes, 6) motivations.
Theme *Thinking skills: Draw inferences; generalize from details; synthesize various elements*	How does the author communicate the theme through the development of setting, characters, and plot? What passages and details in the story best express the main theme?	Look for passages and details from each main part of the story or drama that express theme.

Focused Re-reading of Poetry		
Focus and Thinking Skills	**Questions to Ask**	**Finding Textual Evidence**
Persona (the poet's "voice") *Thinking skills: Analyze; draw inferences*	How does the persona relate to the subject, mood, and theme of the poem?	Look for specific examples that show the persona's involvement and reveal attitudes.
Meter and rhyme *Thinking skills: Analyze meter and rhyme; synthesize to assess their effect*	How do the meter and rhyme affect the rhythm and mood of the poem?	Look for metrical patterns and rhyme schemes from several places in the poem.
Sound devices, such as alliteration, assonance, onomatopoeia *Thinking skills: Analyze language; classify types of sound devices; draw inferences about their meaning and effect*	What sound devices are in the poem? What effect do they have?	Look throughout the poem for examples of sound devices in relation to other elements of the poem.
Theme *Thinking skills: Draw inferences; generalize from details; synthesize various elements*	How does the poet communicate the theme through the details of the poem?	Look for passages and details from throughout the poem that express theme.

3. Synthesis: Evaluate the Text

By now you may have encountered the "new book" that close reading often reveals, a text with layers of meaning. On later re-readings, you can stand back from the text and begin to see it from a critic's point of view. Following are some of the criteria by which any great work of literature, or classic, is usually judged. When you evaluate a literary work, nonfiction or fiction, consider the following characteristics.

Some Characteristics of Great Literature
• Explores great themes in human nature and the human experience that many people can identify with—such as growing up, family life, personal struggles, or war
• Expresses universal values—such as truth or hope—to which people from many different backgrounds and cultures can relate
• Conveys a timeless message that remains true for many generations of readers
• Presents vivid impressions of characters, settings, and situations that many generations of readers can treasure
• Demonstrates outstanding and inventive understanding of important aspects of humanity and society

The chart below shows some questions you can ask—and answer with evidence from the text—when you are evaluating a text.

Questions for Evaluating a Text	
Informational Text	How effectively has the writer • presented a clear explanation on a topic of value • used examples and other supporting details • accurately conveyed information • structured the explanation • used language and style to add clarity and life • presented an unbiased view • engaged the reader
Argumentative Writing	How effectively has the writer • presented a clear position or claim on a subject of importance • used examples and other details to support claims • accurately conveyed information • addressed counterclaims • used logic • covered the topic in sufficient depth and breadth • been fair-minded • structured the argument • used language and style to add clarity and life • convinced you
Fiction and Drama	How effectively has the writer • drawn well-rounded characters worth getting to know • developed and paced a plot • set mood and tone • used language • structured the story • developed a meaningful theme
Poetry	How effectively has the poet • used (or not used) rhyme • created stunning word pictures • used figurative language • structured the poem • expressed an otherwise inexpressible idea

USING TEXTUAL EVIDENCE

Prove it! Anytime you write a literary analysis, informational text, or argument, you will be expected to prove your main idea or claim. You draw the **textual evidence** for that proof from the collection of details you have mined during your close readings.

During your close readings, you gathered evidence by taking notes from the work itself. These notes may have included descriptive passages, lines of dialogue, narrative details, facts, examples, statistics, and other kinds of details. In drafting an analysis of a text or in piecing together an informational or argumentative text from several sources, include the evidence in a way that will convince readers of your main idea or claim.

Strengthen your arguments by using relevant quotations from your text or texts that support a point. Work them smoothly into your writing and punctuate them correctly. The following guidelines show how to work textual evidence into a written analysis. They use examples from a literary analysis on a short story by Marjorie Kinnan Rawlings called "A Mother in Mannville."

Guidelines for Using Direct Quotations in a Literary Analysis

1. Always enclose direct quotations in quotation marks.
2. Follow the examples below when writing quotations in different positions in the sentence. Notice that quotations in the middle or end of a sentence are not ordinarily capitalized.

Begins Sentence	"He wore overalls and a torn shirt," observes the narrator (323).
Interrupts Sentence	In his "grave gray-blue eyes," the narrator sees a rare and precious quality (325).
Ends Sentence	The narrator feels that Jerry's integrity makes him "more than brave (325)."

3. Use ellipses—a series of three dots (. . .)—to show that words have been left out of a quotation.

   "For a moment, finding that he had a mother shocked me . . . and I did not know why it disturbed me" (327).
4. If the quotation is four lines or longer, set it off by itself without quotation marks. Indent one inch on the left and leave space above and below it.

   > And after my first fury at her—we did not speak of her again—his having a mother, any sort at all, not far away, in Mannville, relieved me of the ache I had had about him. . . . He was not lonely. It was none of my concern. (328)

5. After each quotation cite the page number of the text in parentheses. The citation usually precedes punctuation marks such as periods, commas, colons, and semicolons. For plays or long poems, also give main divisions, such as the act and scene of the play or the part of the poem, plus line numbers.

Following are examples of using textual evidence in a different kind of writing—an informational research report on the lost city of Atlantis. The sources are indicated in parentheses and would be keyed to a works-cited page at the end of the report.

Examples of Using Textual Evidence in an Informational Report

1. Use a quotation to finish a sentence you have started.

   Example   Photographs taken in 1977 of underwater stones are believed to "bear the mark of human handiwork" (Whitney).

2. Quote a whole sentence. If you omit words from a sentence, indicate the omission with an ellipsis, a series of three dots (. . .).

   Example   "He suggests that the structures match the description in Plato's Dialogue Critias . . . and that the high mountains of Atlantis are actually those of the Sierra Morena and the Sierra Nevada" (Shermer).

3. Quote four or more lines from a source. For a quotation of this length, skip two lines and set the quotation as a block indented one inch on the left. You do not need quotation marks for such an extended quotation.

   Example   Here is how Plato describes the downfall of Atlantis in the dialogue called *Timaeus:*
   > Some time later excessively violent earthquakes and floods occurred, and after the onset of an unbearable day and a night, your entire warrior force sank below the earth all at once, and the Isle of Atlantis likewise sank below the sea and disappeared. (1232)

4. Quote just a few words.

   Example   According to Plato, in an "unbearable day and a night" Atlantis was destroyed (*Timaeus* 1232).

5. Paraphrase information from a source.

   Example   "Although many have dismissed Atlantis as a myth, some 50,000 volumes have been written to describe and locate it." [Original]
   Curiosity about Atlantis and efforts to locate it gave rise to some 50,000 books on the topic ("Greek Backs Plato Theory"). [paraphrase]

For informational and argumentative texts, including research reports, be sure to verify factual evidence in your sources for accuracy.

Verifying Factual Evidence

- Locate at least two sources that contain the same basic facts.
- Skim each source for specific details, such as dates, locations, and statistics.
- If the specific details in both sources agree, you can probably rely on their accuracy.
- Watch for discrepancies in broader concepts, such as in the sequence of events or in the relationship between cause and effect.
- If you discover discrepancies, use a third source to determine which source is likely to be more accurate.

COMPARING TEXTS

Another way to achieve a deep understanding of a text is to compare it to another text. You can compare and contrast literary texts in many ways. You could, for example, do a close reading of two (or more) texts using any of the same focus points outlined on pages 142–146, and then compare and contrast the way each text addresses that focus point. Following are just a few of many examples.

Two or More Texts of This Type	Focus Points to Compare and Contrast
Short stories	Structure (use of chronological order or flashbacks), theme, plot, character development, point of view, setting, style
Poems	Role of persona, figurative language, rhyme and meter, theme
Biographies	Details of life that are emphasized or omitted in each version; overall sense of person's character and motivation
Informational Texts	Structure, point of view, importance of main idea, support for main idea, language and style, author's purpose, accuracy of information, possible bias
Argumentative Texts	Structure, point of view, significance of main claim, quality of supporting details for claims, logical reasoning, accuracy of information, possible bias, language and style, conclusions

The following chart shows additional ways to compare and contrast texts to deepen your understanding of them.

Types of Texts to Compare	Questions for Comparing Texts
Texts in different forms or genres (such as stories and poems, historical novels and fantasy stories, short stories and novels)	• How is the approach to theme and topic similar in both forms? • How is the approach to theme and topic different in the two forms or genres? • How does their form or genre make these texts unique?
Fictional portrayal of a time, place, or character and a historical account of the same period	• How do authors of fiction use or alter history?
Modern work of fiction versus traditional sources	• In what ways does the modern work draw on themes, patterns of events, or character types from myths, traditional stories, or religious works? • How is the modern work turned into something new and fresh?

continued

Types of Texts to Compare *(cont.)*	Questions for Comparing Texts *(cont.)*
Texts from the same era that approach themes differently	• What was the purpose of each text? • What was the writer's frame of reference or worldview? • Whom was the writer addressing ?
Texts from different eras	• What does each text reveal about social attitudes during the time in which it was written?
Different texts by the same author	• What themes appear repeatedly in works by this author? • What changes in style and/or theme, if any, are apparent in later works by the author compared to earlier works?

Comparing Texts in Different Mediums "Texts" do not necessarily need to be written pieces. In fact, comparing texts in different mediums—such as print, audio, and video—can lead to valuable insights.

The following chart shows some questions to ask when comparing and contrasting texts in different mediums.

Reading a Story, Drama, or Poem	Listening to or Viewing an Audio, Video, or Live Version of the Text
• When you read the text, what do you see in your mind's eye? How do you picture the visual images, the characters, and the setting? • What do you hear—what do the characters' voices sound like? • What are the sounds in the setting? • What can you experience reading a text that you cannot experience when viewing or listening to an audio, video, or live version of the text?	• When you listen to an audio version of the text, what do you experience in comparison to when you read it? Are any elements more vivid? less vivid? • When you view a video version of the text, what do you experience in comparison to when you read it? • What can a video provide that a written text cannot? • How does the experience of a live performance differ from reading a text? • What can a live performance offer that reading a text cannot? • How faithful to the original text is the audio, video, or live version? If it differs in significant ways, why do you think the directors and actors made the choices they did to change it?

You know the techniques writers use to make an impression and impact. They include provocative language, narration that can get inside of characters' heads, and plenty of room for the readers' imaginations to fill in visual and auditory details. Understanding the "tools of the trade" of different mediums can help you make clear comparisons and contrasts.

Techniques of Audio	Techniques of Video	Techniques of Stage
• Actual voices and other sounds in the setting • Possibility of music to help create mood • Room for imagination to fill in visual aspects	• Representation of all sounds and visuals; little left to the imagination • Lighting, sound recording, camera angles, color, focus, and special effects all shape the visual message • Use of background music to help create mood • Editing techniques that place one scene next to another to make a comment	• Representation of some sounds and visuals within the limited scope of the stage • Stage directions that tell characters how to interact in each scene • Lighting and other special effects • Live actors creating a sense of immediacy • Use of music

Sometimes you may be asked to **compare a single scene in two different mediums.** For example, a chilling scene in the book *To Kill a Mockingbird* centers on the shooting of a mad dog by mild-mannered lawyer Atticus Finch. If you read that scene carefully in the book and then compared and contrasted it to the same scene in the movie version of the book, you could evaluate what is emphasized or absent in each treatment of the scene.

Sometimes you may be asked to **compare multiple versions of a story, drama, or poem in different mediums.** How does the stage version of *To Kill a Mockingbird* differ from both the print and movie versions? How do the film and stage versions offer different interpretations of the original text?

AUTHOR BIOGRAPHIES

Akhil Reed Amar After completing law school and spending one year as a clerk for Supreme Court Justice Stephen Breyer, Amar took a position as a professor at Yale University and Yale Law School in 1985. Among his many books about the Constitution and legal procedures, the one that has reached the widest audience is *America's Constitution: A Biography.* In response to the observation that even students in classes studying the Constitution rarely read the entire document, Reed commented, "The running joke is that reading the thing would only confuse the students."

Jack Balkin A professor at Yale Law School, Jack Balkin has written about many topics, but he has a special interest in the legal aspects of new information technology. "The Internet is a significant target of regulation, and that raises all sorts of free-speech problems." Balkin has served as director of the Information Society Project at Yale, which describes itself as "an intellectual center addressing the implications of the Internet and new information technologies for law and society."

Christopher Buckley As the son of William Buckley, one of the country's leading conservatives and the publisher of *National Review*, Christopher Buckley grew up surrounded by politics. "I cast my first vote on my father's lap in 1960, for Richard Nixon, in the voting booth. I was eight. . . . I suppose it was voter fraud, technically. It was very exciting." Though he has called himself a "hack novelist," he has had an impressive career. Besides writing essays for the *National Review,* he served as chief speechwriter for Vice President George H. W. Bush, has written at least eight satirical novels (many of which are about politics), and has frequently contributed humorous pieces to the *New Yorker.*

Richard Buskin A professional freelance writer, Richard Buskin has written more than twenty nonfiction books. Among the most successful of these have been memoirs he has co-authored with celebrities, including ones by singer Sheryl Crow and comedian Phyllis Diller. He has also written numerous music and film reviews and other articles.

Stephen L. Carter On his Web site, Stephen Carter wrote that "As far back as I can remember, I have loved putting words together on a page." Since becoming a professor at Yale Law School in 1982, he has been a prolific writer. He has authored professional papers, newspaper columns, nonfiction books, and at least four suspense novels. His best-known nonfiction book is *Reflections of an Affirmative Action Baby,* published in 1991. In it, Carter describes how affirmative action benefited him, as well as other middle-class African Americans, while arguing that the program has done little to help those who need it most.

Craig Crawford While still in school, Craig Crawford began his life in the political world, serving as a page for Florida Republican Senator Ed Gurney. A few years after graduating from Stetson University College of Law in Gulfport, Florida, he entered journalism and became a successful writer and television commentator. In 2005, he started a popular blog on politics called *Trail Mix*.

Michael A. Fletcher Since he began working on the *Washington Post* in 1995, Michael Fletcher has served five years as the national race relations reporter, a White House correspondent, and a national economics correspondent. Fletcher has been a guest on both radio programs, such as National Public Radio's *Talk of the Nation,* and television programs, such as Black Entertainment Television's *Lead Story.* His book with Kevin Merida about Clarence Thomas grew out of a 2002 magazine story they wrote about the justice. They decided to write the book when, at a party, someone mentioned Thomas's name, and a "raging debate was kindled."

David Gergen Few people in recent years can match David Gergen's wide-ranging career in politics, government, and journalism. While mostly working for Republicans, including positions in the administrations of presidents Nixon, Ford, Reagan, and as a campaign adviser to George H. W. Bush, he also served under Clinton and has held various nonpartisan positions. For example, he has been a senior political analyst at CNN. In 2006, he took a position as a professor at the Center for Public Leadership at the Harvard Kennedy School.

Alexander Hamilton As one of the leading advocates for ratification of the Constitution and as the first Secretary of the Treasury, Alexander Hamilton argued that the federal government should actively support economic growth. His political rivalry with Thomas Jefferson led to the establishment of the first political parties in the United States. He died in 1804 from a gunshot wound after a duel with his political opponent Aaron Burr.

Lee Hamilton A good enough basketball player in high school and college to be inducted into the Indiana Basketball Hall of Fame, Lee Hamilton chose a career in law and politics. Beginning in 1964, he served for 34 years as a Democratic representative from Indiana and became a widely regarded expert on national security and foreign affairs. After leaving Congress, he became director of the Center on Congress at Indiana University. In a radio interview, Hamilton summarized one lesson from his time in Congress: "What has impressed me over the years is the sheer complexity and difficulty of governing this country."

James Huffman Author of more than 100 articles and chapters on legal topics, James Huffman spent most of his career teaching at or as dean of the

Lewis and Clark Law School in Portland, Oregon. He has held a variety of positions on boards and commissions, and received fellowships from the Heritage Foundation and the Hoover Institution. He ran unsuccessfully for the U.S. Senate as a Republican in 2010.

John Kennedy Born into a politically powerful Massachusetts family, John Kennedy was only 29 years old when he was first elected to the House of Representatives in 1947. A few years later, while serving as senator from Massachusetts, John Kennedy worked with his speechwriter Ted Sorensen to write a book highlighting examples of senators who had taken brave political stands throughout American history. The book, *Profiles in Courage,* became a best seller and won a Pulitzer Prize in 1957. In 1960, Kennedy became the youngest person ever elected president (though Theodore Roosevelt was younger when he assumed office). Kennedy was assassinated in Dallas, Texas, on November 22, 1963.

Abraham Lincoln People who knew Abraham Lincoln said that everything he read was for the purpose of making him a better politician. Mostly self-educated, his intense study of the language of Shakespeare and the King James translation of the Bible made him into one of the most elegant writers and speakers among all American presidents. Lincoln loved humorous anecdotes, and sometimes frustrated his cabinet members with his willingness to entertain them with stories before getting down to business.

Vachel Lindsay Born in Springfield, Illinois, in 1879, Vachel Lindsay grew up under the shadow of Abraham Lincoln. As a poet, Lindsay traveled widely, giving recitations of his poetry to all who would listen. Through his energetic performances, he "persuaded the tired businessman to listen at last." He called his style of poetry "singing poetry," because he meant it to be sung—or chanted or shouted—with great emotion.

Dahlia Lithwick Born in Ottawa, Canada, Dahlia Lithwick came to the United States to attend Yale University and Stanford Law School. She developed a successful career as a legal correspondent, working primarily for *Newsweek* and *Slate.* She once suggested that she would like a nominee for the Supreme Court who was a "cross between Rachel Maddow [a liberal host of a news show] and Emma Goldman [an anarchist of the early 1900s]."

Thurgood Marshall Born in Baltimore in 1908, Thurgood Marshall grew up in a working-class family. He began his career as a civil rights lawyer almost immediately after graduating from Howard University School of Law. His success in challenging laws requiring racial segregation reached its high point with the *Brown v. Board of Education* decision in 1954. In 1967, he was confirmed as the first African American to serve on the Supreme Court. He served on the court until 1991, when he retired.

David Mason A professor of literature and writing at Colorado College, David Mason was selected as Colorado Poet Laureate in 2010. One of his best-known works is *Ludlow.* This novel is written in verse and tells the story of a miners' strike in Colorado that began in 1913 and resulted in as many as 200 deaths, including the massacre of approximately 20 miners and their wives and children. In 2007, *Contemporary Poetry Review* selected *Ludlow* as the best book of poetry for the year.

Kevin Merida In 1990, Kevin Merida was part of a team of journalists at the *Dallas Morning News* that were finalists in the Pulitzer Prize competition for their reporting on wars around the world. This was the first of several awards and other recognitions that he has won. In 2000, he was named the National Association of Black Journalists (NABJ) "Journalist of the Year." Three years later, he won a first-place award from the NABJ for commentary. Merida has served as the associate editor for the *Washington Post.*

Eric A. Posner A law professor at the University of Chicago, Eric Posner is a frequent contributor to both scholarly and popular publications. His 2011 book, co-authored by Adrian Vermeule, *The Executive Unbound: After the Madisonian Republic,* argues that the increasing complexity in the world since the Constitution was written has made a stronger executive branch inevitable.

Ronald Reagan After a successful career as a movie actor, Ronald Reagan entered politics and won the election as governor of California in 1966 at age 45. Fourteen years later, he was elected to the first of two terms as president. Noted for his skill as a speaker, his self-confidence, and his humor, one of his best-known quips came barely two months after taking office in 1981. After being shot in the side in an attempted assassination, Reagan was rushed to the hospital. When his wife arrived, he reportedly told her, quoting boxer Jack Dempsey, "Honey, I forgot to duck."

Franklin Roosevelt In 1921, the year he turned 39, Franklin Roosevelt was diagnosed with polio. He was soon paralyzed from the waist down. Historians have speculated about the impact that battling the illness and meeting with others facing similar challenges had on Roosevelt. It might explain why, even though he was born into a wealthy New York family and was a cousin of President Theodore Roosevelt, he was able to connect so well with the "common man." He served as president from 1933 to 1945, and led the country during the Great Depression and World War II.

Rudy Ruiz In 1995, Rudy Ruiz co-founded Interlex, which he describes as "one of the nation's leading advocacy, cause-related, corporate social marketing agencies," and became its president. Since then, he has also started *redbrownandblue.com,* a Web site that provides news and commentary with a multicultural emphasis; hosted *Adelante America,* a nationally syndicated radio program; and contributed commentary to several outlets, including *CNN.com.*

Linda Sánchez Born and raised in southern California, Linda Sánchez graduated from law school and became a labor and civil rights lawyer before entering politics. She was first elected to Congress in 2003. Among her best-known initiatives in Congress has been to lead an investigation into how the National Football League's pension plan treats retirees who suffered injuries while playing. In 2006, Sánchez was named the funniest celebrity in Washington during a charity fund-raiser.

Loretta Sánchez A native of southern California, Loretta Sánchez received her MBA and worked as a financial manager and consultant before entering politics. Though originally a Republican, her disagreements with the party over social issues led her to switch parties in the mid-1990s. She won her first election to Congress in 1996. In an election with nearly 100,000 votes cast, she won by a margin of fewer than 1,000 votes. In Congress, Sánchez has focused on military and national security issues, and has developed a reputation as a forceful, and sometimes blunt, speaker.

Sonia Sotomayor In August 2009, Sonia Sotomayor became the 111th person to serve on the Supreme Court, and the first Hispanic. She was born and raised in New York City. After graduating from law school, she held various positions both in the private sector and as assistant district attorney. In 1992, President George H. W. Bush appointed her to federal district court. Her most famous case as a judge prior to joining the Supreme Court came in 1995, when she ended a seven-month baseball strike by ordering the owners to negotiate with the players.

Leslie Stahl While serving as a White House correspondent in the 1980s and 1990s, Leslie Stahl learned the power of television. "When the pictures are emotional and powerful and when you are saying something that conflicts with them, the messages aren't married; the pictures will drown out what you say." This helped politicians who were good in front of a camera, such as President Ronald Reagan, and hurt those who were not, such as Vice President Dan Quayle. In 1991, she joined the CBS television news program *60 Minutes* and soon became one of the country's best-known journalists.

Clarence Thomas As a small child, Clarence Thomas lived with his family in the small community of Pin Point, Georgia. At age seven, after his father had left the family and a fire had left them homeless, Thomas's mother sent him to live with her father in Savannah, Georgia. Thomas gives great credit to his grandfather for being a positive influence in his life. After attending law school and working mostly in the public sector, Thomas was nominated to the Supreme Court in 1991. After a bitter confirmation battle, he was approved by a vote of 52 to 48.

Helen Thomas In 1942, Helen Thomas began her career in journalism, carrying story manuscripts from writers to editors in a newspaper office in Washington, D.C. She remained in the newspaper business, most notably as a White House correspondent, until 2010. Long a respected journalist who was known as the "First Lady of the Press," she regularly had the honor of marking the close of presidential news conferences with "Thank you Mr. President." She retired in response to the widespread outrage resulting from critical comments she made about Israel.

Alexis de Tocqueville Born into an aristocratic family in France in 1805, Alexis de Tocqueville became famous in the United States for his two-volume book *Democracy in America,* published in 1835 and 1840. Tocqueville wrote his book after visiting the United States to study the American prison system, at that time considered an innovative way to handle criminals. Tocqueville also wrote significant books about politics in Algeria and about the French Revolution.

Shankar Vedantam Best known as a science reporter, Shankar Vedantam has written books about a range of topics, including politics, history, and psychology. *The Ghosts of Kashmir* is a collection of short stories about the Indian-Pakistani conflict. *The Hidden Brain* explains how people unconsciously make decisions about politics and economics. *When Violence Masquerades as Virtue* is a history of terrorism.

George Washington When George Washington was born in 1732, the British colonies in North America were firmly part of the British Empire. As a young man, Washington served in the British army, and led troops that clashed with French forces in 1754 in what was later considered the first battle of the French and Indian War. From this military experience, Washington's career unfolded. He is almost unanimously regarded as the most influential president in the history of the United States.

Michael Zuckerman After working on a senatorial campaign, one of his supervisors described Michael Zuckerman as "one of the most hardworking, dedicated, smart, positive, helpful, kind people you will ever have the privilege of working with." He describes his skills as "political organizing, analysis, and speechwriting." He began working as research assistant for David Gergen in 2010 and became an associate at The Boston Consulting Group in 2012.

Acknowledgments

Text Credits

"America's Most Notorious Lobbyist" by Leslie Stahl. From Jack Abramoff: The Lobbyist's Playbook. © November 6, 2011. CBS NEWS ARCHIVES.

"American People Hire Lobbyist" from *The Onion*. Reprinted with permission of THE ONION. Copyright © 2011, by ONION, INC. www.theonion.com.

"As He Shall Judge Necessary" by Akhil Reed Amar. From AMERICA'S CONSTITUTION by Akhil Reed Amar, copyright © 2005 by Akhil Reed Amar. Used by permission of Random House, Inc.

"Citizens as Powerful Lobbyists" by Lee Hamilton. ©2005 Lee Hamilton. Reprinted by permission of the author.

"The Courage to Compromise" by John F. Kennedy. From *Profiles in Courage*. Copyright © 1955, 1956, 1961 by John F. Kennedy. Copyright renewed © 1983, 1984, 1989 by Jacqueline Kennedy Onassis. Foreword copyright © 1964 by Robert F. Kennedy. Reprinted by permission of HarperCollins Publishers.

"Dream in Color" by Linda Sánchez, Loretta Sánchez, and Richard Buskin. From DREAM IN COLOR by Congresswomen Linda and Loretta Sánchez with Richard Buskin; Foreword by Nancy Pelosi. Copyright © 2008 by Linda Sanchez and Loretta Sanchez. By permission of Grand Central Publishing. All rights reserved.

"Friends and Foes on the Supreme Court" by Kevin Merida and Michael A. Fletcher. From SUPREME DISCOMFORT: THE DIVIDED SOUL OF CLARENCE THOMAS by Kevin Merida and Michael A. Fletcher, copyright © 2007 by Kevin Merida and Michael A. Fletcher. Used by permission of Doubleday, a division of Random House, Inc.

"A House Divided Against Itself?" by David Gergen and Michael Zuckerman. From cnn.com, September 28, 2011, © 2011 Time Inc. Used under license. CNN and Time Inc. are not affiliated with, and do not endorse products or services of Perfection Learning.

"The Inevitability of the Imperial Presidency" by Eric A. Posner. From The Washington Post, © April 22, 2011. The Washington Post. All rights reserved. Used by permission and protected by the Copyright Laws of the United States. The printing, copying, redistribution, or retransmission of the Material without express written permission is prohibited.

"Legal Ethics," by Sonia Sotomayor. From The New York Times, June 4, 2009 © 2009 The New York Times. All rights reserved. Used by permission and protected by the Copyright Laws of the United States. The printing, copying, redistribution, or retransmission of this Content without express written permission is prohibited.

"Life in the Senate" by Stephen L. Carter. From Bloomberg View. June 8, 2011. Used with permission of Bloomberg L.P. Copyright © 2012. All rights reserved.

"Listen Up, Mr. President" by Helen Thomas and Craig Crawford. Reprinted with the permission of Scribner, a Division of Simon & Schuster, Inc., from LISTEN UP, MR. PRESIDENT: EVERYTHING YOU ALWAYS WANTED YOUR PRESIDENT TO DO AND KNOW by Helen Thomas and Craig Crawford. Copyright © 2009 by Helen Thomas and Craig Crawford. All rights reserved.

"The President as Teacher-in-Chief" by Rudy Ruiz. From CNN.com, September 8, 2009, ©2009, Cable News Network, Inc. All rights reserved. Used by permission and protected by the Copyright Laws of the United States. The printing copying, redistribution, or retransmission of this Content without express written permission is prohibited.

"Song of the Powers" by David Mason. From THE COUNTRY I REMEMBER (Brownsville, Oregon: Story Line Press). Copyright © 1996 by David Mason. Used with the permission of the author.

"Supreme Courtship" by Christopher Buckley. From SUPREME COURTSHIP by Christopher Buckley. Copyright © 2008 by Christopher Taylor Buckley. By permission of Grand Central Publishing. All rights reserved.

"The Sword and the Robe" by Thurgood Marshall. Excerpted from *Thurgood Marshall: His Speeches, Writings, Arguments, Opinions, and Reminiscences* edited by Mark V. Tushnet. Copyright © 2001 by Mark V. Tushnet. Used with permission of Lawrence Hill Books.

"Trust in the Supreme Court" by Dahlia Lithwick. From Slate, © July 20, 2011. The Slate Group. All rights reserved. Used by permission and protected by the Copyright Laws of the United States. The printing, copying, redistribution, or retransmission of the Material without express written permission is prohibited.

"Wanted: More Judicial Activism!" by James Huffman. Reprinted with permission of Hoover Institution, Stanford University. Copyright © 2011.

Photo and Art Credits